Contents

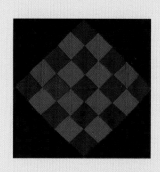

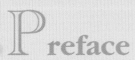

Preface

Vintage Quilts
Identifying, Collecting, Dating, Preserving, and Valuing

This is a comprehensive guide to collecting antique quilts for the novice as well as the sophisticated and experienced collector. Quilt historians and appraisers Sharon Newman, Bobbie Aug, and Gerald Roy, curator of the prestigious Pilgrim/Roy collection, wrote this guide.

Age, pattern, style, size, fabrics, colors, construction techniques, and the quiltmaker and place of origin when available, are used to identify over 600 quilts, quilt tops, and blocks. A specific value or range is given for each. Quilt tops and blocks were included because we have observed a recent passion for collecting these in addition to quilts. Hopefully, you will discover a broad assortment of quilts, tops, and blocks that cover a wide range of values. You should find quilts that you see every day as well as those that are extremely rare and expensive.

It should be noted that all of the textiles in this book, except for two or three family quilts, were purchased by the authors. We shopped the retail market in our own vicinities, regionally, and nationally and made these purchases. We have experienced the values listed in these pages! However, since these quilts were all purchased over a long period of time, our over fifty cumulative years of professional quilt appraisal experience made it possible for us to ascertain current values for our textiles.

Each quilt, top, and block is pictured in color. Where helpful, we have indicated specific information about each item that collectors should find of interest.

Information is presented about structuring a comprehensive quilt collection. Suggestions for storage, display, preservation, and conservation are also included.

The values in this book are retail values and should be used only as a guide. They are not intended to set prices, which vary from one region of the country to another and are affected by the condition of the textile as well as supply and demand and the local and national economy. The only true guide to determining value is between a buyer and a seller. Neither the authors nor the publisher assume responsibility for any losses that might be incurred as a result of consulting this guide.

Introduction

Hundreds of thousands of quilts were made during the past two centuries by American quiltmakers. The need for warm covering was a motive for quiltmaking in the earliest times, but the beauty created by many of the quiltmakers has intrigued collectors for many years. Quilts of all patterns and styles continue to turn up in estate sales and regional auctions. The current interest in quiltmaking by a million and a half Americans has renewed a parallel interest in the quilts of the past. Interest in antique quilts has resulted in statewide quilt search days and the publication of state history and statistics about antique quilts. Fabrics and quilts designed from antique patterns are frequently published in magazines sold internationally.

During the past quarter century, American quilts have received recognition worldwide as the cultural and artistic value of quilts continues to be explored. Quilts can be purchased in many places. The flea market find is rare in this day of well-published information about all quilts, but bargains are still to be found in local auctions, estate sales, and antique stores. Vendors of antique quilts can be found in the many quilt shows throughout the country. Internet quilt dealers are plentiful and the quilts can be viewed at all times of the night and day.

Cover design: Beth Summers
Book design: Holly C. Long

COLLECTOR BOOKS
P.O. Box 3009
Paducah, Kentucky 42002-3009
www.collectorbooks.com

Copyright © 2002 Bobbie Aug, Sharon Newman, Gerald Roy

The current values in this book should be used only as a guide. They are not intended to set prices, which vary from one section of the country to another. Auction prices as well as dealer prices vary greatly and are affected by condition as well as demand. Neither the authors nor the publisher assumes responsibility for any losses that might be incurred as a result of consulting this guide.

Searching For A Publisher?

We are always looking for people knowledgeable within their fields. If you feel that there is a real need for a book on your collectible subject and have a large comprehensive collection, contact Collector Books.

VINTAGE Quilts

IDENTIFYING, COLLECTING, DATING, PRESERVING & VALUING

Bobbie Aug,
Sharon Newman
&
Gerald Roy

COLLECTOR BOOKS
A Division of Schroeder Publishing Co., Inc.

Consider the condition of the quilts that you are willing to accept in your collection. Many quilt collectors start by rescuing worn quilts. The fabrics, patterns, and quilting designs can be used for display, study, or replication. More experienced collectors prefer to buy quilts that are in excellent condition and thereby eliminate the need for time-consuming and expensive restoration or conservation. Generally, quilts in excellent condition will cost more to purchase than quilts in poor condition. We recommend that you purchase quilts in the best condition that you can afford.

Quilt collecting came into vogue during the 1920s and has steadily grown in popularity. The first bit of advice for quilt collectors is the same as for collectors of any other item: Buy what you like and buy the best you can afford. Consider making a plan for the theme of your collection. It is more desirable to assemble a unified collection, rather than just accumulating a group of quilts.

Closely examine any quilt you desire to purchase. Have the quilt held up vertically so that you can see the way the quiltmaker arranged the elements of the design. Look for patterning in scrap quilts. Look for symmetry in appliqué and quilting designs. Look for the innovative way a setting or border changes the quilt. And again, determine the overall condition of the textile.

Some of the most interesting collections are those that represent the personal tastes and interest of the collectors. Collections can be as unique and individual as the collectors themselves.

Collecting by Color

Some collectors choose quilts of a particular color or color combination. Blue and white quilts of any pattern or age are the most collected of all quilts. Red and white is a close second. Red and green with yellow or orange also comprise a category of very collectible quilts. Sometimes collectors focus on a color, such as pink, and only collect quilts that are primarily that color.

Collecting by Pattern or Style

Log Cabin, Nine Patch, and stars are probably the most recognizable patterns and many examples still can be found by collectors. Nine Patch blocks can be the subject for a collection. The little block was reputed to be made as a first block for children, and can be found in all decades of patchwork. A similar design is the uneven Nine Patch, commonly called Puss in the Corner.

A collector could define a collection by purchasing quilts made from Mountain Mist patterns or patterns designed by Ruby McKim or Nancy Page.

There are literally thousands of quilt patterns so you are only limited by your imagination.

Style might indicate a technique such as broderie perse or appliqué. Or, style might reference a certain arrangement such as four block or medallion. Also, we might think in terms of style meaning theme, like patriotic or centennial.

Refer to each individual section, for example, Log Cabin Quilts or Double Wedding Ring, where specific patterns or styles, but different examples are shown together.

Collecting by Special Visual Elements

Finding a quilt with great graphics, innovative techniques, artistic color choice, unusual setting choice, or special finishing techniques will suit the collector of this kind of quilt. Not the ordinary of any pattern, but a maverick of some detail, is what they seek. Collectors of these elements find quilts with a look that is unique. Quilts with only chintz fabrics would be a good example of special elements. Quilts that pertain to mourning or coffins would be another category.

Quilts from different regions of the United States often have different characteristics. Pennsylvania quilts are a good example. With Amish, Mennonite, and Quaker quiltmakers and quiltmakers of German heritage, the quilts vary in color, design, fabric, pattern, and finishing technique.

Collecting Quilts by Age

Study quilts of the type you want to collect in museums, quilt shows, and publications. Note the typical coloring for the age of the quilt. Study the patterns, settings, and borders. Look at the quilting designs. Educate yourself about the quarter century style changes and choose the era in which you want to collect quilts.

Setting boundaries on the age of the quilts collected will define the collection. Collections containing examples of only nineteenth century quilts or only twentieth century quilts are possible. Depending on the use of the collection, quilts may represent every decade of American quiltmaking. A large variety of quilts were made in the fourth quarter of the nineteenth century, including pieces, appliquéd, and crazy quilts; therefore a large collection could consist of quilts from that 25 year period. Turn of the century quilts are prized by some collectors. The distinctive two-color prints and limited pallet did not create a limit for the quiltmakers of the time.

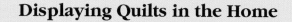

Displaying Quilts in the Home

One of the oldest methods of displaying the very best quilts in the house is to put them on beds. Arrange to remove the quilts before the bed is used. Quilts exhibited on racks and in decorative wall hangers should be examined carefully as the quilts might exhibit uneven discoloration if not moved regularly. Any direct contact with sunlight or unsealed wood should be avoided.

Using antique quilts to decorate your home has been in vogue for many years. Quilts on display are frequently of interest to visitors. Use quilts as textile art in many different rooms. Protect each quilt from bright light and place it away from cooking areas where grease and moisture are more prevalent. Prepare the quilt to hang by stitching on a sleeve.

Providing Safe Storage for Your Quilts

Storage must be arranged for your collection. Quilts not being displayed need to be protected from acids, dust, light, and the stress of being stacked. Air circulation should be provided. Storage should be in an area with even, moderate humidity and temperature (not the attic or the basement). Embrittlement is very destructive and can be avoided or postponed for decades. This condition is caused by great fluctuation of temperature, humidity, pollution in the air, sunlight, and soil. If quilts are stored in an area with high humidity, check often for signs of mold and mildew. Overly dry conditions can cause dehydration and breaking of the fibers. When a humidifier is needed for humans, quilts will benefit as well.

Cleanliness and good housekeeping will insure that no pests get into your quilts. Food stains and other soil provide nutrients for insects and mold. Mothballs and other chemicals are no longer recommended because they can cause damage to textiles and are toxic to humans. Cedar, another popular home remedy, does not provide a safe deterrent to insects. Cedar is also bare wood, and a source of acid deterioration for any fabric stored on its surface. Monitor pest activity on a regular schedule with your usual cleaning.

When folding quilts for storage, acid-free paper should be used by placing sheets of the paper between the layers of the quilt and scrunched up in the folds of the quilt in order to prevent the quilt from touching itself and prevent "pancake" folds or creases in the textile. Fold the quilt into the size that will fit on a finished shelf or in a finished cabinet. Cover the shelf with unbleached muslin or acid-free tissue paper. Refold the quilt about every three months. Do not stack quilts more than two deep. The weight of the fabric and batting will be hard on the quilts at the bottom. Restack when the quilts are refolded.

Acid-free storage boxes can be purchased from archival storage materials suppliers. These are opaque, expensive, and need to be replaced about every three to five years. In semi-arid regions such as Nevada, Arizona, and Colorado, quilts can safely be stored in polypropylene or polyethylene (plastic) storage containers. This type of material is inert and will not give off harmful gasses that could damage textiles. Unbleached muslin is used to loosely line the container in order to "wick" out any moisture that might have accumulated on the quilt or in the box. The tops of these containers are not air tight, and so circulation is provided. The sizes available include underbed storage and two or three quilt sizes. The boxes can be stacked and no damage occurs to the quilts.

Rolling quilts for storage saves space and is more economical than purchasing acid-free boxes. Probably for these reasons, museums frequently roll quilts around dowels or carpet tubes attached to the wall. Rolling, however, puts tension on every square inch of the cloth. In addition, the batting is pulled to one side of the quilted area and visually distorts the surface of the quilt. We recommend avoiding rolling if at all possible.

Attaching a Sleeve

Prepare and sew a sleeve to the top edge of the back of the quilt in this manner: Cut a 9" wide strip of muslin the width of the quilt, less two inches. On each end, turn under another ¼", then turn under another ¼". Stitch to hem both ends. Fold the fabric in half lengthwise with wrong sides together. Stitch. Press the seam allowance open and center the seam against the back of the sleeve. Hand stitch the top edge of the sleeve with thread to match the front of the quilt. Use a running stitch, taking small stitches (¼" – ½") on the front and large stitches (½" – 1") on the back. On the lower edge of the sleeve, fold the crease up ½" and sew the sleeve to the back of the quilt in the same manner as the top. The extra fullness will prevent the quilt from being stretched by the lathe strip or drapery rod used to mount the quilt on the wall.

Protecting Your Collection

A quilt collection of even a few quilts should be covered with insurance. Companies who write homeowner's insurance vary in the amount of coverage provided in the basic plan. Check with your insurance agent to make sure your collection is protected.

A certified appraiser of quilts should be contacted to prepare an appraisal for each of the quilts in your collection. A knowledgeable appraiser should also be able to evaluate your quilts as a collection.

Amish quilts made prior to WWII have a distinctive style and appearance, regardless of the state in which they were made, or the Amish order of the quiltmaker. The quilting patterns are an important design element as is the way the colors chosen interact across the quilt's surface. Known provenance or family history is highly valued when these quilts are offered for sale.

Mennonite quilts are thought of in much the same way, although not quite as distinctive in fabric choices and they do not demand prices as high as that of the Amish-made quilts.

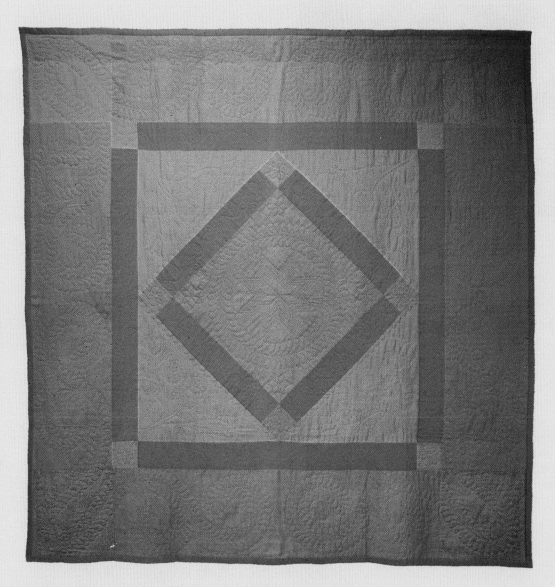

Amish Center Diamond, 78" x 78", circa 1890, Lancaster County, Pennsylvania, wool, excellent workmanship, excellent condition, $10,000.00.

A.

B.

A. Amish Sunshine and Shadow, 73" x 76", circa 1890, wool, excellent workmanship, excellent condition. It is unusual and noteworthy to have baskets quilted in border. $8,000.00 – 10,000.00.

B. Amish Center Diamond, 77" x 77", circa 1930, Lancaster County, Pennsylvania, wool and wool crepe, excellent quilting, excellent condition, $8,000.00 – 10,000.00.

C. Amish crib quilt, 35" x 35", circa 1890, wool, excellent condition, $1,000.00 – 1,200.00.

C.

A. Amish Center Diamond, 80" x 80", circa 1890, Lancaster County, Pennsylvania, wool, heavily quilted, rare pattern without corner blocks, visually exceptional, excellent condition, one of the best examples of this type with regards to its color interaction, $8,000.00 – 10,000.00.

B. Lancaster Amish Bars, 72" x 78", circa 1910, Pennsylvania, excellent condition. The early patterns found in Amish quilts are Center Diamond Bars and Sunshine and Shadows. Quilting designs are important because they are so obvious. $6,300.00 – 6,500.00.

A.

B.

A.

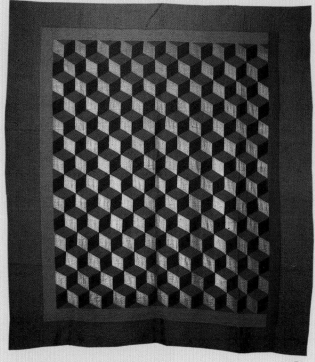

B.

C.

A. Amish Bars, 78" x 76",
circa 1890, Lancaster County,
Pennsylvania, wool, heavily
quilted, bordered on three sides,
initialed "A.S.," very rare
"floating bars," $4,500.00.

B. Amish Tumbling Blocks,
72" x 78", circa 1940, Ohio,
excellent workmanship, excellent
condition, beautifully quilted,
$4,000.00 – 5,000.00.

**C. Doors and Windows
Blocks,** 68" x 75", blocks circa
1920, quilted 1991, made from
blocks found in an Iowa estate
by Dorothy Bond and quilted by
Sara Miller, Mary Slabaugh, Susie
Ropp, and Tanya Gilement.
Finding quilts made by authors
such as Dorothy Bond with
documentation as to their
origin is unusual and may add
value. $1,400.00 – 1,600.00.

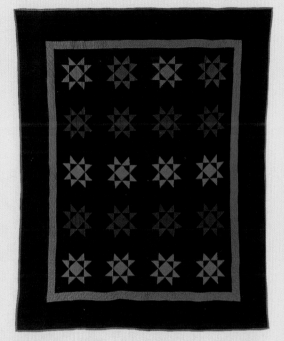

A.

B.

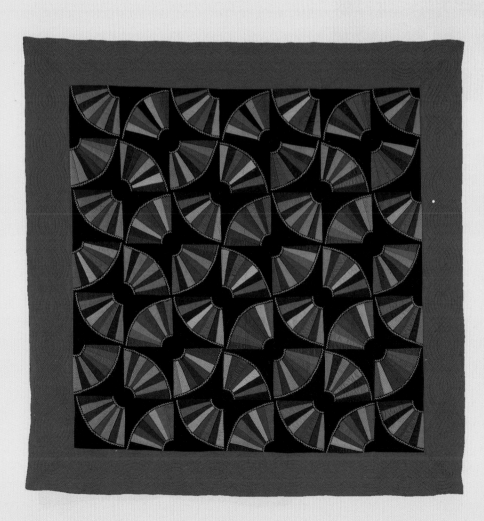

A. Amish Baskets,
84" x 67," circa 1930,
Holmes County, Ohio,
very unusual set, great
color arrangement,
$3,000.00 – 4,000.00.

B. Amish Stars, 68" x 80",
circa 1920, Holmes
County, Ohio,
$3,400.00 – $3,600.00.

C. Amish Fans, 79" x 79",
circa 1900, Lancaster,
Pennsylvania, extremely
rare example, exceptionally
fine workmanship,
excellent condition,
$6,000.00 – 8,000.00.

C.

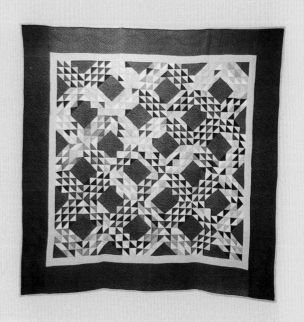

B.

A.

A. Amish Chimney Sweep,
66" x 92", circa 1920, Holmes
County, Ohio, excellent
workmanship, excellent
condition, extraordinary,
$2,800.00 – 3,200.00.

B. Amish Ocean Waves,
75" x 75", circa 1920, Ohio,
yellow applied binding, pink
backing, quilted in black and
white quilting thread, feathered
vine quilted in the border, cross
tulips in centers, excellent
condition, $3,500.00 – 3,700.00.

C. Amish Triple Irish Chain,
78" x 90", circa 1900, Ohio,
great quilting, excellent
condition, $2,000.00 – 2,500.00.

C.

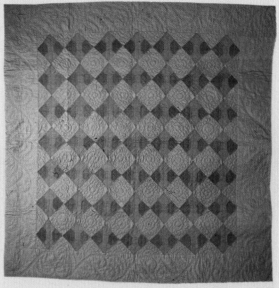

A.

B.

A. Amish Four Patch in Uneven Nine Patch, 60" x 62", circa 1910, made by Emma Gengerick Ohio, unusual, excellent condition, $1,800.00 – 2,200.00.

B. Amish Bow Tie, 69" x 69", circa 1900, Mifflin County, Pennsylvania, silk file and wool, very beautiful color, subtle fine quality, excellent condition, $2,800.00 – 3,000.00.

C. Kentucky Amish Wool, circa 1900, poor condition due to fabric loss, value less than $200.00.

C.

A.

B.

C.

A. Garden Patch,
69" x 83", dated 1895
and 1910, Indiana, ini-
tials "DES" are in the
quilting,
$1,800.00 – 2,000.00.

**B. Amish Pinwheel
Stars,** 76" x 84", dated
1909, Ohio, $900.00 –
1,100.00.

C. Amish Buggy Robe,
55" x 55", circa 1910,
Midwest, wool, rare,
$3,500.00.

A.

B.

A. Bricks, 72" x 75", circa 1900, Old Order Mennonite or Amish, wool, Pennsylvania, heavily quilted, unusual pattern, print backing, back brought around to finish front edge, excellent condition, visually superb, $5,000.00.

B. Brickwork Hired Hands Amish Quilt, 38" x 73", circa 1940, Ohio, heavily quilted, excellent workmanship, excellent condition, rare, $3,000.00.

C. Amish Brickwork, youth size, 68" x 51", circa 1920, Ohio, applied binding, moderate to heavy quilting, excellent condition, $3,800.00 – 4,000.00.

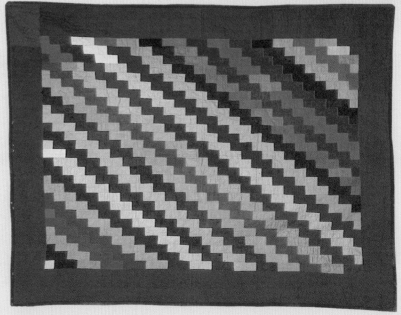

C.

B.

A.

A. Amish Bricks,
46" x 57", circa 1920,
Arthur, Illinois, excellent
condition,
$900.00 – 1,100.00.

B. Amish Bricks,
46" x 57", circa 1920,
Arthur, Illinois, youth size,
wool, very graphic,
excellent condition,
1,000.00 – 1,200.00.

**C. Amish Zigzag or
Stairway to Heaven,**
70" x 76", circa 1910,
Holmes County, Ohio,
cotton, excellent
condition,
$2,100.00 – 2,300.00.

C.

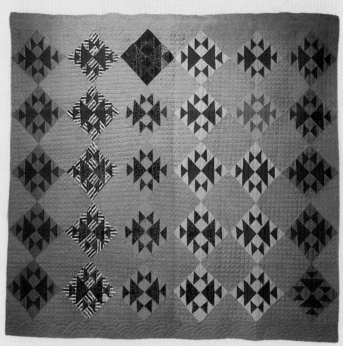

A.

B.

C.

A. Amish Old Maid's Puzzle,
76" x 81", circa 1920, Arthur,
Illinois, wool, excellent
condition, $1,800.00 – 2,000.00.

B. Uneven Nine Patch,
72" x 89", circa 1890, Mifflin
County, Pennsylvania, wool,
minor damage, heavily quilted
in one inch grid, back to front
edge finish,
$1,200.00 – 1,400.00.

C. Amish Nine Patch,
 64" x 88", circa 1910, Mifflin
County, Pennsylvania, wool,
excellent condition,
$1,400.00 – 1,600.00.

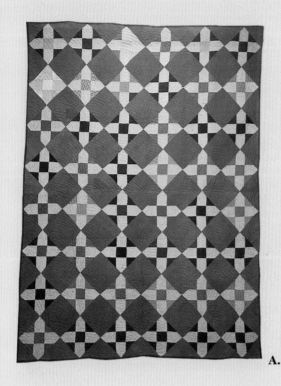

A.

B.

A. Amish Double Cross, 60" x 80", circa 1910, Arthur, Illinois, excellent condition, $700.00 – 900.00.

B. Amish Jacob's Ladder, 69" x 80", circa 1940, Ohio, cotton, excellent condition, $1,400.00 – 1,600.00.

C. Amish Four Patch in Nine, 70" x 70", circa 1915, Mifflin County, Pennsylvania, excellent condition, $1,500.00 – 1,700.00.

D. Amish Boston Corner Variation, 69" x 79", circa 1900, Canada, wool top, cotton back, excellent condition, $1,200.00 – 1,400.00.

C.

D.

A.

A. Appliqué Christmas Quilt
(Oakleaf and Reel), 101" x 101",
1848, Vermont, stamped ink
names and date 1848, each signature personalized with Christmas verses, excellent
workmanship, excellent
condition, extraordinary and
rare, $10,000.00.

**B. Broderie Perse Summer
Spread,** 99" x 105", circa 1800,
Massachusetts, linen, very good
condition, $7,000.00.

B.

A.

B.

C.

A. Lily, 98" x 106", circa 1820, New York, excellent workmanship, excellent condition, beautifully quilted, chintz border, rare quilt, $6,500.00 – 7,500.00.

B. Prince's Feather, 86" x 88", circa 1860, Ohio, appliqué and reverse appliqué with eagles, birds, and peacocks, along with pots of flowers, made by Mary Price (1825 – 1916), Barnesville, Ohio, for Frances Fowler, $3,500.00 – 4,500.00.

C. Detail of Prince's Feather, elaborately quilted, tiny buttonhole stitch.

A.

B.

A. Mennonite Appliqué and Reverse Appliqué Papercut Designs, 88" x 88", circa 1870, Lancaster County, Pennsylvania, excellent condition, $3,500.00 – 4,000.00.

B. Detail of Mennonite Appliqué quilt.

C. Cockscomb Variation, 81" x 92", circa 1840, Germantown, Ohio, appliqué and reverse appliqué, extraordinary, excellent condition, $5,000.00 – 6,000.00.

D. Detail of Cockscomb Variation. Clamshell quilting and double line quilting.

C.

D.

A.

B.

A. Thistle and Plume Appliqué with Birds, 88" x 90", circa 1860, Berks County, Pennsylvania, excellent condition, $3,500.00 – 4,000.00.

B. Cherries Appliqué, 87" x 87", circa 1865, Pennsylvania, excellent condition, $3,500.00 – 3,800.00.

C. Peony Appliqué, 76" x 100", circa 1860, New York, excellent condition, $3,500.00 – 4,000.00.

C.

A.

B.

C.

A. Carolina Lily, 80" x 98", circa 1850, pineapple border, Garden Maze setting, $3,400.00 – 3,600.00.

B. Carolina Lily with Leaf, Vine, and Flower Border, circa 1860, New York, heavily quilted in clamshell pattern, two different appliqué blocks in upper and lower corners on left, extraordinary, excellent workmanship, excellent condition, $2,800.00 – 3,000.00.

C. North Carolina Lily, 77" x 90", circa 1860, heavily quilted, piped edge finish, excellent condition, $1,400.00 – 1,600.00.

A.

B.

C.

A. Tulip Appliqué, 88" x 91", circa 1840, Ohio, heavily and beautifully quilted, excellent condition, $3,500.00 – 4,500.00.

B. Appliqué Tulip with Tulip Bud Border, 76" x 76", circa 1860, Pennsylvania, signed, "Rosemary's Quilt, made by Grandma Yost," probably Mennonite, excellent "as new" condition, remarkably quilted in feather wreaths, etc., never used, $2,200.00 – 2,400.00.

C. Appliqué Birds, Leaves, and Tulips, 72" x 85", circa 1850, heavily quilted in single and double parallel lines, red applied binding, slightly faded, $2,200.00 – 2,400.00.

A.

B.

A. Whig Rose, 84" x 84", circa 1860, Pennsylvania, interesting borders, note the attention to detail on the corners, excellent workmanship, excellent condition, $1,600.00 – 1,800.00.

B. Floral Wreath Appliqué, Pennsylvania, paper-cut border, circa 1880, excellent condition, moderate amount of quilting, $1,600.00 – 1,800.00.

C. Prairie Rose, 68" x 92", 1854, made by Elizabeth Dunlap in Dubuque, Iowa, excellent workmanship, excellent condition, rare, $3,000.00 – 3,200.00.

C.

A.

B.

C.

A. Red and Green Appliqué, 76" x 76," circa 1865, made by Lavinia Mikesell Mowdy Dilts, born April 1841 in Indiana. The quilt was given to George Washington Dilts, her son. She received a $1,200.00 per year pension following the death of her husband, Lewis Dilts who died of dysentery contracted during service in the Civil War. Original design featuring hearts, a motif used often for wedding quilts and quilts celebrating births, $1,800.00 – 2,000.00.

B. Cutwork Appliqué, 71" x 67", circa 1920, Vermont, unusual, excellent condition, $1,600.00 – 1,800.00.

C. Paper-cut Original Design Appliqué and Reverse Appliqué Summer Spread, 88" x 88", circa 1860, Pennsylvania, nine blocks, all but center square contains doves as part of the design elements, excellent condition, $1,200.00 – 1,400.00.

A.

B.

A. Harrison Rose Variation, 76" x 91", circa 1850, $3,400.00 – 3,600.00.

B. Whig Rose Variation, 88" x 89", circa 1840, Pennsylvania, excellent workmanship, excellent condition, $3,000.00 – 3,200.00.

C. Mennonite Whig Rose, 90" x 90", circa 1885, Pennsylvania, backing on this quilt is in bars, $3,000.00 – $3,200.00.

C.

A.

B.

C.

A. Whig Rose, 90" x 90", circa 1920, Pennsylvania, $3,300.00 – 3,500.00.

B. Appliqué Original Pattern, circa 1860, New England, quilted in clamshell design, excellent condition, $800.00 – 1,000.00.

C. Grapes, Vines, and Feathers, 92½" x 96", circa 1850, Northern Kentucky, excellent condition, $3,600.00 – 3,800.00.

B.

A.

A. Tulip, 99" x 101", circa 1840, Ohio, heavily quilted with all different sampler patterns, Some staining and wear. Although it would have been easier to appliqué the blocks, they're pieced. $3,600.00 – 3,800.00.

B. Appliqué Original Design Summer Spread, 68" x 68", circa 1860, Ephrata, Pennsylvania, four block Tulip and Fern, excellent condition, $450.00 – 600.00.

C. Rose of Sharon Variation Summer Spread, 73" x 92", circa 1860, Pennsylvania, borders on only two sides, excellent condition, $400.00 – 600.00.

C.

31

A.

B.

C.

A. Oak Leaf and Reel Variation, circa 1860, Ohio, excellent condition, $750.00 – 850.00.

B. Whig Rose Appliqué, 92" x 92", circa 1860, Pennsylvania, Mennonite, some fabric loss, very rare on dark blue background, $1,600.00 – 1,800.00.

C. Center Medallion Appliqué 70" x 77", 1890, Pennsylvania, very rare, possibly a buggy robe. The story that accompanies this quilt is that it was made as a gift to an old order Mennonite bishop when leaving his community to go to a new community. $7,000.00 – 9,000.00.

A.

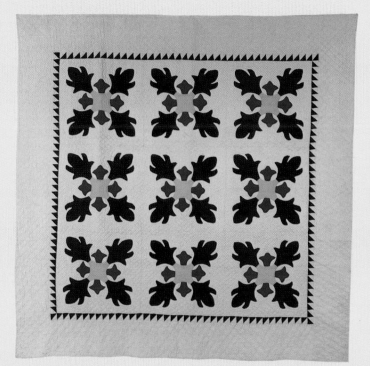

B.

A. Eagle Appliqué, 86" x 84",
circa 1875, Pennsylvania,
excellent condition,
$800.00 – 1,000.00.

**B. Red and Green Pineapple
Variation,** 78" x 78", circa 1860,
Pennsylvania, excellent
workmanship, excellent
condition, $1,800.00 – 2,000.00.

**C. Pineapple Appliqué
Variation,** 98" x 100", circa
1835, Ohio, excellent
workmanship, excellent
condition, $4,400.00 – 4,600.00.

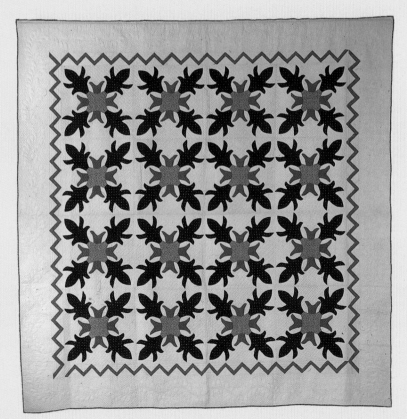

C.

A.

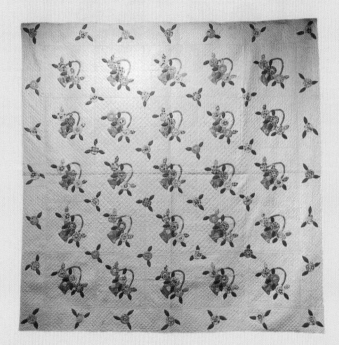

B.

C.

A. Pot of Flowers Appliqué, 1917, Pennsylvania, dated in quilting, Ely and Walker Fabric, style is identical to those made in previous times, excellent workmanship, excellent condition, $800.00 – 1,000.00.

B. Baskets of Flowers, 91" x 91", circa 1925, New Hampshire, excellent workmanship, excellent condition, $650.00 – 700.00.

C. Appliqué French Rose, circa 1940, Midwest, excellent condition, $650.00 – 750.00.

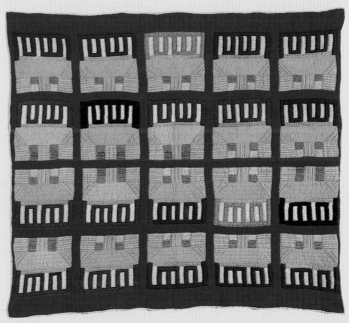

A.

B.

C.

A. Houses, 73" x 60",
circa 1940, Grand Rivers,
Kentucky, very unusual color
and set. The blocks are set in
this quilt so that two rows are
upright on each side when
the quilt is on a bed.
$1,200.00 – 1,500.00.

B. Democratic Rose,
66" x 76", 1932 – 1938, dates
1932 and 1938 embroidered
on opposite corners, straight
grain applied binding,
excellent condition,
$500.00 – 600.00.

**C. Appliqué Flower Basket
Kit,** 74" x 90", circa 1940,
hand quilted, bias binding
edge finish, excellent
condition,
$1,400.00 – 1,600.00.

A.

A. Wildflowers, 78" x 94," circa 1930, pastel prints and solids were particularly popular with quiltmakers between 1920 and 1940 and many of the quilts can be dated by the colors used, quilts like this one that have been made with unusual patterns are collectible, $1,200.00 – 1,400.00.

B, Floral Medallion, 81" x 89", circa 1930, published pattern, well executed, heavily quilted and beautifully embroidered button-hole stitch appliqué, excellent condition, $500.00 – 700.00.

C. Appliqué Flowers in Basket, 78" x 90", circa 1940, Ohio, French knots, button-hole stitch and embroidered summer spread, excellent condition, $400.00 – 600.00.

B.

C.

B.

A.

A. House on the Hill, 60" x 79", circa 1930, excellent condition, $300.00 – 500.00.

B. Marie Webster French Basket, 83" x 84", circa 1920, Claremore, Oklahoma. Marie Webster designed this pattern and several others in the first quarter of the twentieth century. Her patterns and kits were sold nationwide. $800.00 – 1,000.00.

C. Roosevelt Rose, 68" x 84", circa 1920, Missouri. This pattern was published in the 1930s and examples can occasionally be found. The use of the pastel prints from the 1920s and 1930s on black was fashionable. $2,000.00 – 2,200.00.

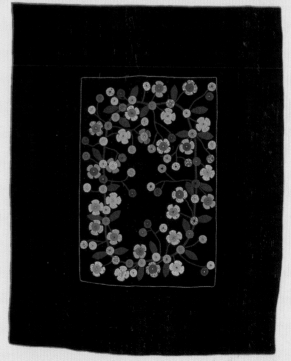

C.

Appliqué and Stuffed Work Quilts

A.

A. Baltimore Album Quilt, 104" x 104", 1847, made for and signed by Georgianna Eltonhead (b. 1830), the daughter of Sarah and Thomas Eltonhead, a watchmaker jeweler and silversmith in Baltimore, other signatures and dates indicate the makers, etc. Mary, Martha and Marie Riley, excellent condition, provenance: Florence Peto, Tenafly, New Jersey, $60,000.00 – 65,000.00.

B. & C. Details of Baltimore Album Quilt. Ribbon embroidery, embroidery, stuff work.

B.

C.

A.

A. Roses and Stuffed Work Appliqué, 84" x 84", circa 1860, heavy ornate quilting, narrow piped border, very fine, excellent condition, $3,600.00 – 3,800.00.

B. Detail of Roses and Stuffed Work Appliqué

B.

Whole Cloth Bride's Quilt, 86" x 86", circa 1830, Stewartsville, Missouri, made by Ms. Litzenberg, heavily stuffed "hearts abound," center panel a basket of flowers, very fine, excellent condition, $10,000.00.

Chintz Medallion Broderie Perse and Patchwork, 76" x 78",
circa 1820, North Carolina, good example of early fabrics and
pattern designs, excellent workmanship, excellent condition,
rare, $5,000.00 – 5,200.00.

A.

B.

C.

D.

A. Touching Stars of Bethlehem,
83" x 108", 1854, Bucks County,
Pennsylvania, dated 1854 and
signed M.G.M., very rare, excellent
condition, quilt has been published
many times, $4,500.00 – 5,000.00.

B. Mariner's Compass, 73" x 80",
circa 1860, blue and white with
beautiful quilting, excellent
workmanship, excellent condition,
extraordinary quilt,
$3,800.00 – 4,500.00.

C. Turkey Track and Dove,
92" x 92", circa 1860, Ephrata,
Pennsylvania, made by Sarah W.
Bounds, appliquéd sawtooth
border, center block a dove in
flight, very rare, excellent condition,
$3,500.00 – 4,000.00.

D. Detail of dove.

A.

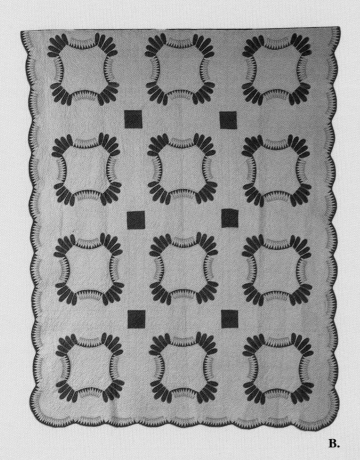

B.

A. Lone Star on Orange with Rosebud Appliqué, circa 1880, Pennsylvania, extraordinary quilting, slightly faded area, $2,800.00 – 3,000.00.

B. Whig's Defeat, 68" x 84", circa 1920, unusual pattern for the pastel colors of this period, excellent workmanship and heavily quilted, $2,800.00 – 3,000.00.

C. Oak Leaf and Reel, 84" x 88," circa 1840, Ohio, red and green quilts are very graphic and collectible. $2,500.00 – 2,800.00.

C.

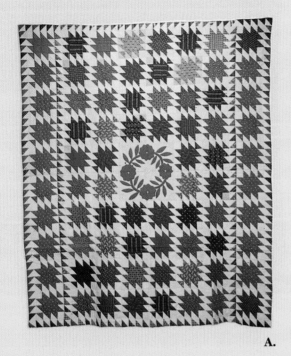

A.

B.

C.

A. Anvil Variation, 65" x 76", circa 1885, Pennsylvania, Rose Wreath appliqué center block and Sawtooth border, rare, excellent condition, $1,800.00 – 2,000.00.

B. North Carolina Lily, 82" x 84", circa 1880, Pennsylvania, excellent condition, $1,600.00 – 1,800.00.

C. Blazing Star with Sawtooth Border on Printed Ground, 84" x 84", circa 1875, Pennsylvania, rare, excellent workmanship, excellent condition, $2,600.00 – 2,800.00.

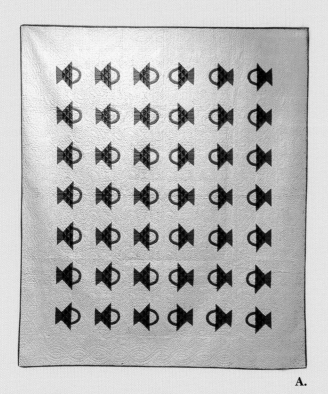

A.

B.

A. Little Baskets, 68" x 78", circa 1880, Ohio, heavily quilted, excellent condition, $1,400.00 – 1,600.00.

B. Rainbow Variation, 68" x 87", circa 1940, made in the Midwest, original design, $800.00 – 1,000.00.

C. Tulip in Vase, 80" x 80", circa 1885, Pennyslvania, red and green solids with yellow print background, unusual appliquéd handles on vase. Backing is pieced in double pink print and green print bars. $900.00 – 1,100.00

C.

A.

A. Basket with Appliqué Leaf Border, 76" x 93", circa 1890, Vermont, very heavily quilted, excellent workmanship, excellent condition, $1,400.00 – 1,600.00.

B. Carolina Lily Medallion with True Lovers Knot in the surrounding areas, 84" x 84", circa 1890, Vermont, excellent condition, $1,000.00 – 1,200.00.

C. The back of the Carolina Lily Medallion is One Patch Bars.

D. Heart appliqué at the lower right corner of back. Some would speculate that this quilt was made as a wedding gift.

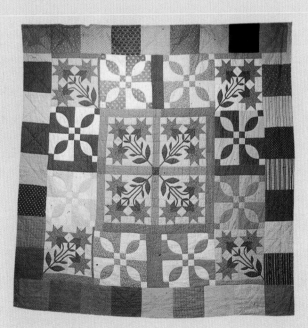

B.

C.

D.

A.

B.

A. Center Medallion Appliqué, 69" x 82", circa 1900, Pennsylvania, very unusual, excellent condition, $650.00 – 800.00.

B. Starflower, 90" x 102", circa 1940, 192 starflowers and 66 appliquéd and embroidered butterflies within the borders, 570 circles buttonhole stitched on the borders, excellent condition, heavily quilted, very fine quilting, $3,800.00 – 4,000.00.

C. Full Blown Tulip, 74" x 88", circa 1860, "Ella Wickham" is stamped on the back of the quilt, excellent condition, $1,600.00 – 1,800.00.

C.

A.

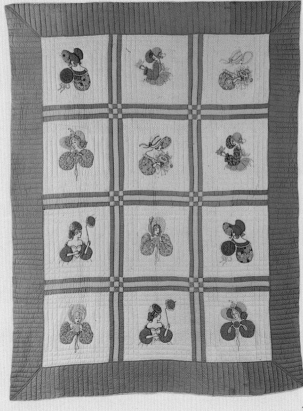

B.

C.

A. Pot of Flowers, 76" x 88,"
circa 1920, Texas, excellent
workmanship, excellent
condition, $400.00 – 600.00.

B. Poster Girl, 74" x 92",
circa 1935, Texas, these
designs were advertised in
needlework catalog of the
mid 1930s, excellent
condition, $500.00 – 700.00.

C. Butterfly, 78" x 80", circa
1935, Indiana, excellent
condition, $350.00 – 550.00.

A.

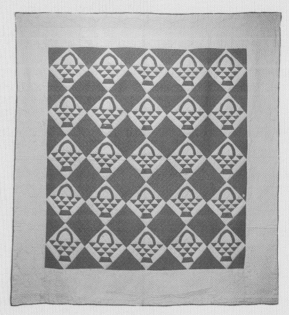

C.

A. Pansies, circa 1870,
very unusual, fair condition,
$400.00 – 600.00.

B. Sunflower Appliqué,
76" x 64", circa 1910,
North Carolina, excellent
condition, $400.00 – 600.00.

C. Mennonite Baskets,
76" x 80", circa 1880,
appliquéd handles, cable
quilting in border,
excellent workmanship,
excellent condition,
$1,100.00 – 1,300.00.

B.

A.

A. Star of Bethlehem,
101" x 104", circa 1820,
Pennsylvania or New York,
chintz squares and triangles
complete the set, woven
tape binding, excellent
condition, rare,
$7,500.00 – 8,000.00.

B. Medallion, 93" x 96",
circa 1800, Massachusetts,
linen and cotton, some
staining and wear,
$600.00 – 800.00.

B.

A.

B.

A. LeMoyne Star, 78" x 84", circa 1880, center medallion on point with Sawtooth, zigzag borders, LeMoyne Star corners, excellent workmanship, excellent condition, $1,600.00 – 1,800.00.

B. Mennonite Eight Pointed Star, 79" x 81", circa 1880, Lancaster County, Pennsylvania, stars with Sawtooth borders in four corners, fans center all four sides in crotch of star blades, embroidered decorative stitches on seams, very strong visually, exhibited and published, excellent condition, rare, $4,500.00 – 5,000.00.

C. LeMoyne Star, 110" x 116", circa 1825, Portsmouth, New Hampshire, signed, "Elizabeth Chase 1796," excellent condition, moderate to heavy quilting, knife edge finish, fine homespun cotton sheeting on back, $6,000.00 – 8,500.00.

C.

A.

B.

C.

A. LeMoyne Star with Diamond Border, 100" x 100", circa 1860, Massachusetts, unusually decorative woven tape binding, quilted in 1" diagonal parallel lines throughout, exciting use of directional (stripe) fabric, excellent workmanship, excellent condition, $2,800.00 – 3,000.00.

B. Touching Stars, 100" x 106", circa 1840, Pennsylvania, fancy woven tape binding, beautifully quilted, excellent workmanship, excellent condition, $4,000.00 – 5,000.00.

C. Sunburst, 85" x 85", circa 1830, Maine, chintz border, excellent condition, $2,500.00 – 3,000.00.

A. Star of Bethlehem, 81" x 80", 1890, Lancaster County, Pennsylvania, nine touching stars beautifully executed, heavily quilted with exceptional quilting, $3,000.00 – 3,200.00.

B. Touching Stars, 80½" x 80½", circa 1870, Pennsylvania, excellent condition, $900.00 – 1,100.00.

C. Amish Blazing Stars Touching, 76" x 78", circa 1920, Indiana, very graphic on dark blue ground, excellent condition, $2,400.00 – 2,600.00.

A.

B.

C.

A.

B.

C.

A. Touching Stars,
72" x 72", circa 1880,
Sawtooth border, piped
edge finish,
$900.00 – 1,100.00.

B. Eight Pointed Star, 70"
x 80", circa 1930, Indiana,
excellent condition,
$600.00 – 800.00.

**C. Six Pointed Stars
Touching,** circa 1930,
Tennessee, diamond areas
between large stars are
filled with patchwork
creating a very different
central design, 12 compass
blocks complete the
set, very unusual,
$900.00 – 1,100.00.

A.

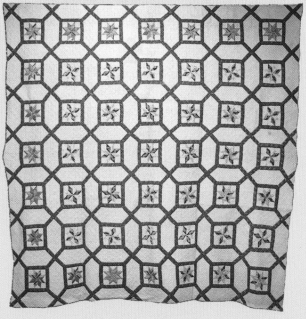

B.

A. Prairie Star, 81" x 81",
circa 1880, Pennsylvania,
$700.00 – 900.00.

**B. LeMoyne Star
Set in a Garden Maze**,
88" x 90", circa 1850,
$2,400.00 – 2,800.00.

C. Evenings Stars,
100" x 108", circa 1840,
Pennsylvania, excellent
workmanship, excellent
quilting, $4,500.00.

C.

A.

B.

A. Variable Star on Point,
76" x 76", circa 1880,
Pennsylvania, very careful
arrangement of blocks to create
symmetry with different fabric
backgrounds and corners,
excellent condition,
$1,600.00 – 1,800.00.

B. Feathered Star, 71" x 85,"
circa 1875, Ohio, very good
craftsmanship, heavily quilted,
unusual sunburst design at
center of stars, along with
pieced border, create a very
graphic quilt,
$1,600.00 – 1,800.00.

C. Feathered Star, 77" x 77",
circa 1880, Vermont, blue and
white quilts and red and white
quilt are the first and second
most popular color combination
with collectors,
$800.00 – 1,000.00.

C.

A.

B.

A. Prairie Star, 68" x 86,"
circa 1890, Indiana,
$800.00 – 1,000.00.

B. Shadow Star, 68" x 80",
1873, signed and dated in
embroidery (both outline and
cross stitch) and stamped with
ink, "Made as Auntie Angeline's
Friendship Quilt," according to
note found with the quilt,
signatures are from the
Burnham family of Essex,
Massachusetts, signature,
provenance, and date adds
value, $700.00 – 900.00.

C. Eight-pointed Star,
62" x 84", 1962,
Bessie Newman, Brownwood,
Texas, fabrics from late 1950s
and early 1960s,
$500.00 –700.00

C.

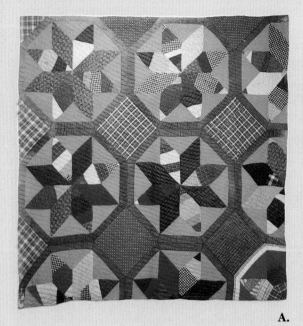

A.

B.

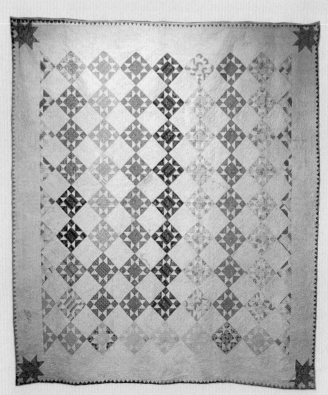

C.

A. String Pieced Star in a Garden Maze, 78" x 82", circa 1910, North Carolina, excellent condition, $400.00 – 500.00.

B. Evening Stars, 106" x 113", 1838, New Jersey, dated 1838 in center and signed Lydia H. Moore, excellent workmanship, excellent condition, $2,400.00 – 2,600.00.

C. Hanging Evening Stars, 82" x 96", 1830, New England, signed and dated 1830, discoloration, $600.00 – 800.00.

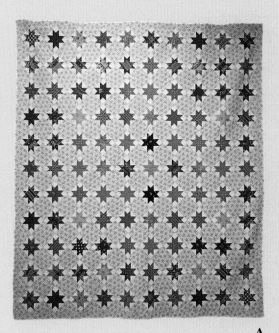

A.

B.

A. Evening Stars, 84" x 96", circa 1850, New Hampshire, center medallion arrangement, $2,400.00 – 2,600.00.

B. Hanging Evening Stars, 84" x 89", circa 1875, Pennsylvania, preprinted patchwork back. The pieced blocks in this quilt are extremely small and therefore, a higher degree of technical difficulty. This adds value. $2,600.00 – 2,800.00.

C. Sawtooth or Evening Star, 70" x 86", circa 1860, Ohio, excellent condition, $900.00 – 1,100.00.

C.

A.

A. Rolling Stone, 71" x 80", circa 1945, Midwest, excellent condition, $350.00 – 500.00.

B. Lone Star on Navy Blue, 80" x 80", circa 1875, rare color use, excellent condition, $800.00 – 1,000.00.

C. Lone Star, 82" x 82", circa 1940, Pennsylvania, excellent condition, $600.00 – 800.00.

B.

C.

A.

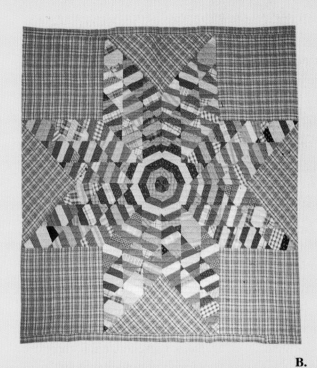

B.

C.

A. Lone Star, 77" x 78", circa 1895, Pennsylvania, print background, excellent condition, $600.00 – 800.00.

B. String Star (plaid between points), 70" x 77½", circa 1910, Midwest, flannel backing, back to front edge finish, moderate/heavy quilting, $600.00 – 700.00.

C. Lone Star, 70" x 78", circa 1890, excellent condition, $600.00 – 800.00.

A.

B.

A. Mennonite Broken Star, circa 1890, Franklin County, Pennsylvania, made by Mrs. Meyers, seven of these quilts are thought to exist, one made for each of the maker's seven children, three are known to exist and are in private collections, excellent in every way, $4,800.00 – 5,000.00.

B. Eight Pointed Star on Pieced Ground, 70" x 80", circa 1940, Michigan, background areas divided diagonally with yellow and blue, very unusual and graphic, excellent condition, $900.00 – 1,100.00.

A. Broken Star, 75" x 87", circa 1935, Michigan, excellent condition, $500.00 – 700.00.

B. Broken Star, 76" x 84", circa 1940, some fading, $400.00 – 600.00.

C. Eastern Star, 75" x 84", circa 1940, excellent condition, $500.00 – 700.00.

A.

B.

C.

A.

A. Nine Patch Flower with Ice Cream Cone Border, 73" x 84", circa 1930, Indiana, heavily quilted, very interesting set forming a large center medallion, excellent condition, $700.00 – 900.00.

B. Star, 66" x 82", circa 1950, Missouri, excellent condition, $300.00 – 500.00.

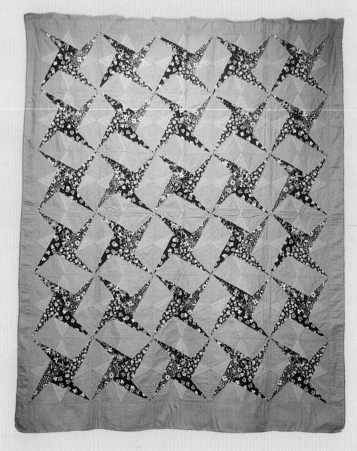

B.

A.

A. Barn Raising Variation,
73¾" x 73¾", 1879, Massachusetts,
inscribed on back: "To A.M.
Herrick from her Mother age
81 1879," silk and velvet,
most extraordinary quilt,
complex color arrangement,
flowers embrodered on
velvet in each center, excellent
workmanship, excellent
condition, the signature
and date add value,
$6,000.00 – 8,000.00.

B. Log Cabin Barn Raising,
80" x 80", circa 1875,
Pennsylvania, excellent
condition, $1,200.00 – 1,500.00.

B.

A. Barn Raising, 73" x 73", circa 1880, Massachusetts, cotton and satin glazed cotton back, $1,600.00 – 1,800.00.

B. Off-center Log Cabin, 86" x 72", circa 1880, Pennsylvania, excellent condition, $1,800.00 – 2,000.00.

C. Barn Raising, 53" x 86", circa 1890, Pennsylvania, silks and satin, excellent condition, $1,200.00 – 1,500.00.

A.

B.

C.

A.

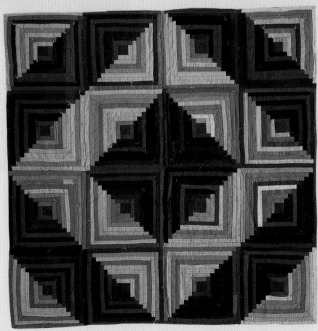

A. Barn Raising Variation, 66" x 74", circa 1870, Lancaster County, Pennsylvania, very unusual set which creates dynamic visuals, rare, excellent condition, $2,500.00 – 3,000.00.

B. Log Cabin Barn Raising, 77" x 78", circa 1915, Oley Valley, Pennsylvania, excellent condition, $350.00 – 450.00.

B.

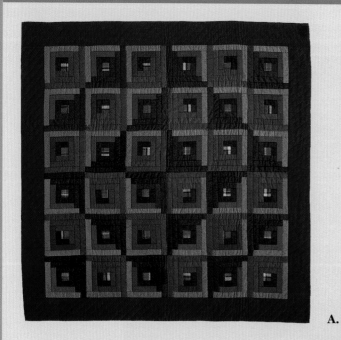

A. Log Cabin Barn Raising Variation, 70" x 70", circa 1890, Pennsylvania, wool. excellent condition, $1,200.00 – 1,500.00.

B. Multiple Barn Raising, 79" x 79", circa 1890, Pennsylvania, wool, multiple barn raising sets create a dramatic graphic quilt, $1,800.00 – 2,200.00.

C. Log Cabin, 61" x 80", circa 1930, New York, unusual set, $1,200.00 – 1,400.00.

A.

B.

C.

A.

A. Pineapple Log Cabin,
78" x 86", circa 1875, Ohio,
wool, note the multiple
borders, unusual,
excellent condition,
$3,800.00 – 4,000.00.

B. Pineapple Variation,
89" x 89," circa 1875,
Pennsylvania, wool and wool
challis, excellent condition,
$2,500.00 – 2,800.00.

B.

A.

B.

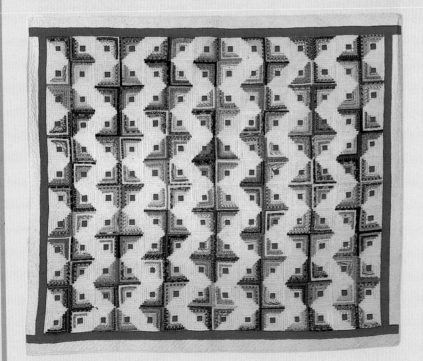

C.

A. Log Cabin Pineapple,
91" x 93", circa 1890, Maine,
excellent workmanship,
excellent condition,
$2,400.00 – 2,800.00.

B. Zigzag Log Cabin,
77" x 68", circa 1900, Missouri, excellent condition,
$900.00 – 1,100.00.

C. Vertical Log Cabin,
98" x 66¾", circa 1890, New
England, excellent condition,
heavily quilted, vertical
settings in Log Cabin quilts
are rare, especially those
with two patterns,
$3,000.00 – 3,200.00.

A.

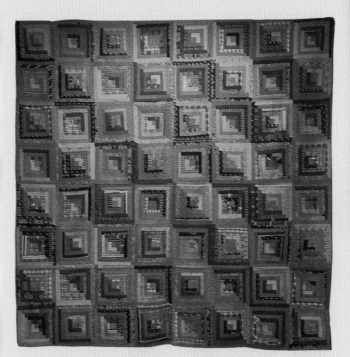

B.

A. Mennonite Log Cabin in Bars Setting, 80" x 88", circa 1880, Pennsylvania, rare setting for Log Cabin blocks, excellent condition with very good quilting, $1,800.00 – 2,000.00.

B. Log Cabin, 94" x 94", circa 1860, Pennsylvania, wool challis, Straight Furrow set, excellent condition, $1,200.00 – 1,400.00.

C. Straight Furrow Quilt Top, 74" x 98", circa 1875, Pennsylvania, cotton, excellent workmanship, excellent condition, $650.00 – 750.00.

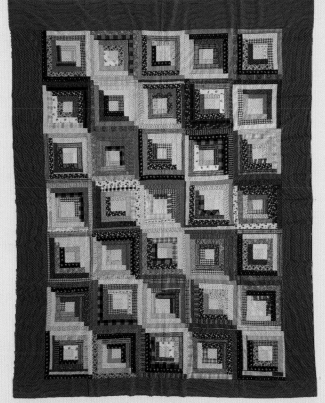

C.

A. Straight Furrow, 68" x 78", circa 1900, Missouri, wool, excellent condition, $300.00 – 400.00.

B. Sunshine and Shadow with Zigzag Border, 60" x 65", circa 1870, made by Rebecsa (Rebexy) Gray in Lincoln, Illinois, extremely fine example, very small pieces, beautifully made of silk and velvet, yellow silk taffeta backing, very good workmanship, $6,000.00 – 7,500.00.

A.

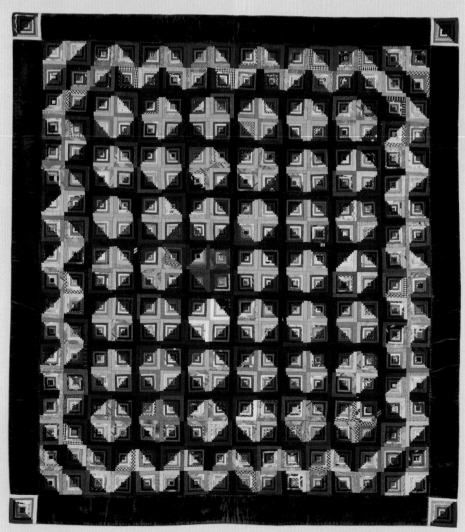

B.

A. Courthouse Steps,
66" x 78", circa 1860,
Michigan, wool challis,
excellent condition,
$1,800.00.

**B. Log Cabin Court House
Steps,** 92" x 96", circa 1885,
Vermont, excellent condition,
$1,200.00 – 1,400.00.

C. Log Cabin, 64" x 74",
circa 1920, Texas, half-square
triangle centers are not usual,
$400.00 – 600.00.

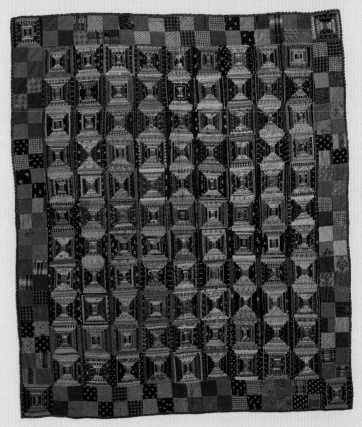

A.

B.

C.

A.

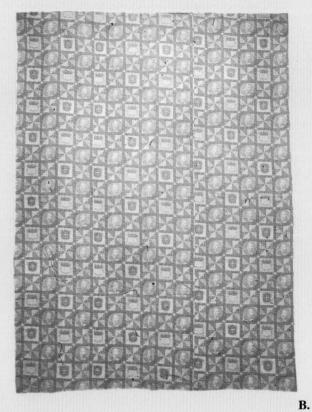

B.

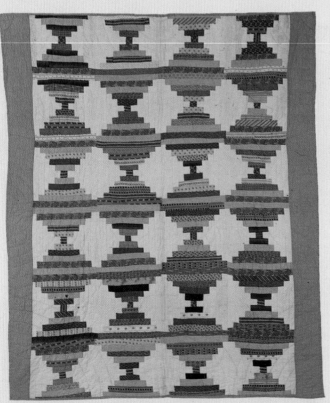

C.

A. Courthouse Steps with Hourglass Centers, circa 1880, Midwest, excellent condition, $650.00 – 750.00.

B. This is the back of the Courthouse Steps quilt listed above. It is Ulysses S. Grant pre-printed patchwork.

C. Courthouse Steps, 76" x 82", circa 1870, Michigan, $500.00 – 700.00.

A.

A. Log Cabin Courthouse Steps, 66" x 79", circa 1900, Pennsylvania, wool, silks, cotton, bordered, excellent condition, $650.00 – 750.00.

B. Log Cabin Dark and Light Variation, 78" x 76", circa 1910, Pennsylvania, wool and cotton, $600.00 – 700.00.

B.

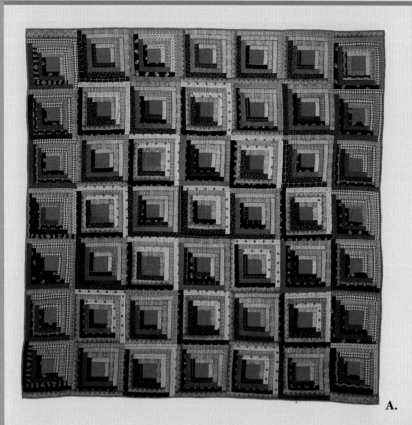

A. Log Cabin Straight Furrow, 89" x 88", circa 1875, Pennsylvania, rare among Log Cabins. large red centers add to overall powerful visuals, excellent workmanship, excellent condition, $2,500.00 – 3,000.00.

B. Hit or Miss Log Cabin, 77" x 77", circa 1910, wool, excellent condition, very graphic, $600.00 – 800.00.

C. Log Cabin Barn Raising, 83½" x 81½", circa 1860, Adams County, Pennsylvania, made by Florence Mae Hart Diehl, excellent condition, $2,800.00 – 3,000.00.

A.

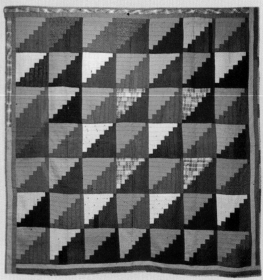

B.

C.

A. Bars, 84" x 87", circa 1820, New England, chintz, back is also pieced in bars, $600.00 – 800.00.

B. Tree Everlasting, 81" x 85", circa 1880, Ephrata, Pennsylvania, Sawtooth border, excellent workmanship, excellent condition, $1,800.00 – 2,000.00.

A.

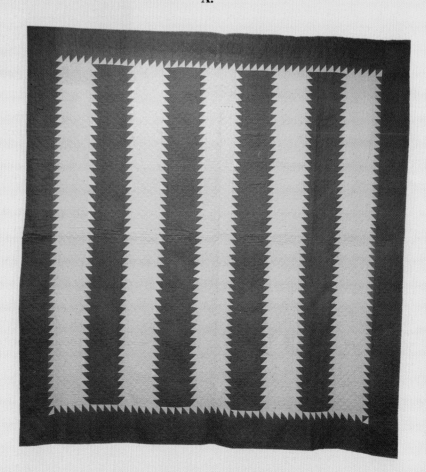

B.

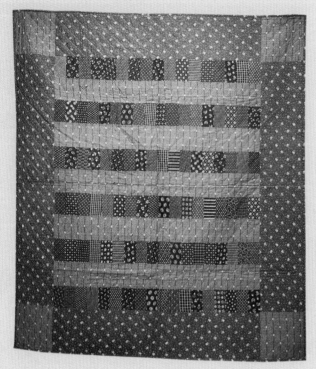

A.

B.

C.

A. Bars Crib Quilt,
51" x 58", circa 1870, back
to front edge finish,
excellent condition,
$950.00 – 1,100.00.

B. Nine Patch in Bars, circa
1880, Pennsylvania, Nine
Patches preprinted
patchwork, excellent
condition, $650.00 – 800.00.

C. Framed Bars, 80" x 84",
circa 1880, Pennsylvania,
very striking Pennsylvania
Dutch, pink, yellow, and
blue, excellent condition,
$800.00 – 1,000.00.

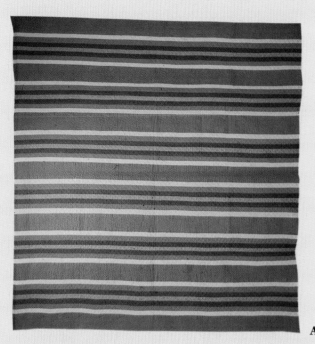

A.

A. Bars, 85" x 88", circa 1880, Pennsylvania, excellent workmanship, excellent condition, $500.00 – 700.00.

B. Purple Triangles, 78" x 81", circa 1890, excellent condition, $600.00 – 800.00.

C. Mennonite Bars, 77" x 80", circa 1920, Pennsylvania, excellent condition, $300.00 – 500.00.

D. Mennonite Bars, 78" x 80", circa 1890, Pennsylvania, two sided, pink/green and pink/red, excellent workmanship, excellent condition, $400.00 – 600.00.

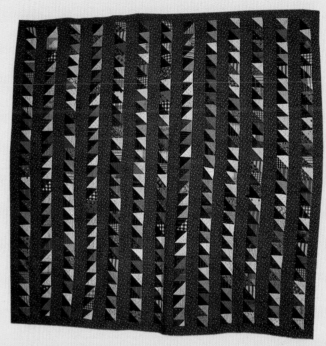

B.

C.

D.

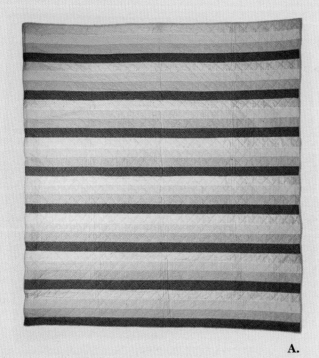

A.

B.

C.

A. Mennonite Bars, 87" x 92", circa 1875, Lancaster County, Pennsylvania, excellent quilting, excellent condition, $900.00 – 1,200.00.

B. Garden Path, 72" x 85½", circa 1900, Texas, $300.00 – 500.00.

C. Tree Everlasting, 70" x 70", circa 1900, $400.00 – 600.00.

A.

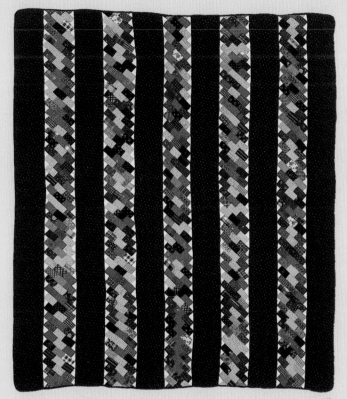

B.

A. Roman Coins, 70" x 84",
circa 1900, Indiana,
$300.00 – 500.00.

B. Stacked Bricks,
71" x 79½", circa 1885,
$800.00 – 1,000.00.

C. Tree Everlasting,
68" x 76", circa 1900, Ohio,
800.00 – 1,000.00.

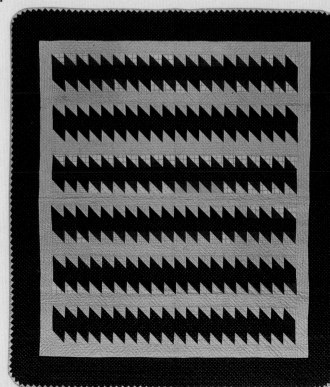

C.

Double Wedding Ring and Pickle Dish Quilts

A. Double Wedding Ring,
64" x 81", circa 1930,
Pennsylvania, very unusual
rings end well within the
quilt edges to create a
floating appearance,
excellent condition,
$400.00 – 600.00.

B. Double Wedding Ring,
78" x 78", circa 1940,
Pennsylvania, rings on
orange inner border are
pink, very unusual, excellent
condition, $600.00 – 800.00.

A.

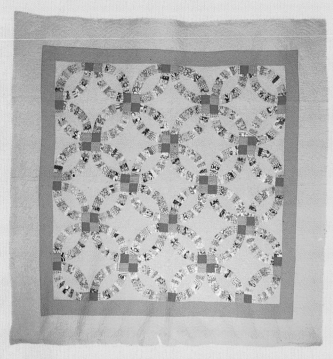

B.

A.

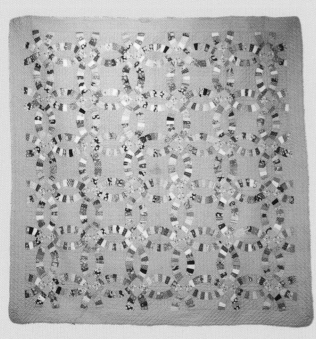

B.

A. Double Wedding Ring,
67" x 80", circa 1920,
Missouri, very graphic,
excellent condition,
$600.00 – 800.00.

**B. Double Wedding Ring
on Yellow Print,** 90" x 90",
circa 1940, unusual border
treatment, very graphic,
$500.00 – 700.00.

C. Double Wedding Ring,
79" x 82", circa 1940,
Missouri, Afro-American,
each ring is 23", applied
binding, very graphic,
$800.00 – 1,000.00.

C.

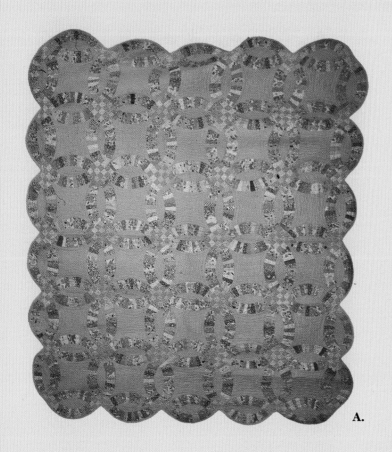

A. Double Wedding Ring, 74" x 86", circa 1920, note the sixteen patch in the centers, unusual, excellent condition, $600.00 – 800.00.

B. Double Wedding Ring, 60" x 78", circa 1930, Missouri, color arrangement causes a strong diagonal design, excellent condition, $600.00 – 800.00.

C. Double Wedding Ring, 63" x 73", circa 1925, Missouri, the appeal is low contrast, creates an allover design, $300.00 – 500.00.

A.

B.

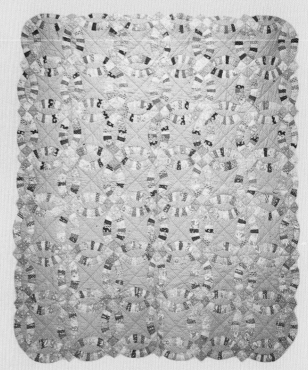

C.

A.

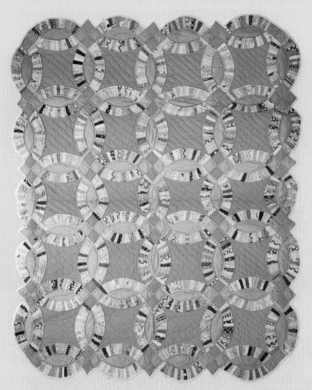

B.

A. Double Wedding Ring,
85" x 87", circa 1930,
Kentucky, border very
unusual, binding frayed,
$650.00 – 750.00.

B. Double Wedding Ring,
45" x 54", circa 1930,
Midwest, making this pattern
smaller increases the
difficulty of the design,
$300.00 – 500.00.

C. Double Wedding Ring,
68" x 79", circa 1920, unusual
printed border, straight grain
binding, $500.00 – 700.00.

C.

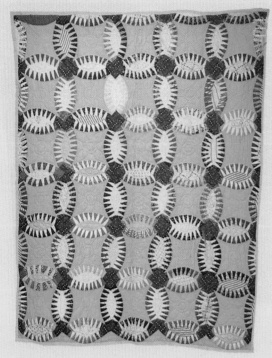

A.

B.

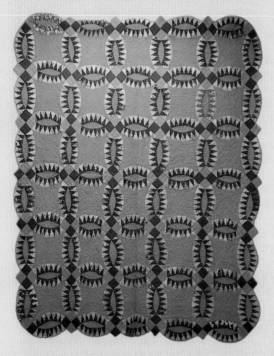

C.

A. Pickle Dish, 71" x 89",
circa 1930, Pennsylvania,
excellent condition,
$750.00 – 850.00.

**B. Pickle Dish or Indian
Double Wedding Ring,**
78" x 78", circa 1845,
fair/good condition,
hand quilted,
$900.00 – 1,100.00.

C. Indian Wedding Ring,
65" x 82", circa 1920,
Tennessee,
$600.00 – 800.00.

A.

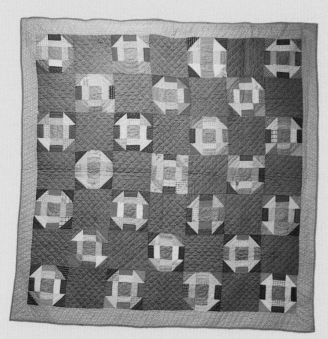

B.

A. Churn Dash,
66" x 74", circa 1890,
Midwest,
$400.00 – 600.00.

**B. Hole in the Barn
Door,** 73" x 75", circa
1910, Midwest,
$400.00 – 600.00.

A.

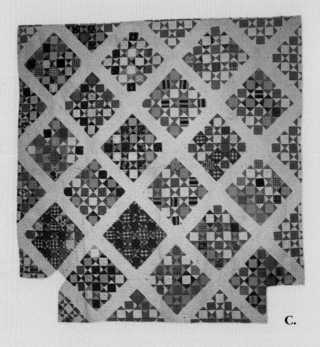

C.

B.

A. Hourglass, 66" x 82", circa 1910, Kansas, excellent condition, $600.00 – 800.00.

B. Hole in the Barn Door, 76" x 86", circa 1885, Massachusetts, made by Jenne Burtner's mother, Mrs. Bradford — she was a direct descendant of Governor William Bradford of first Plymouth Plantation, traditional pattern in unified color and planned scrap setting, $800.00 – 900.00.

C. Broken Dishes Variation, 71" x 71", circa 1870, New England, blocks are set on point, $800.00 – 1,000.00.

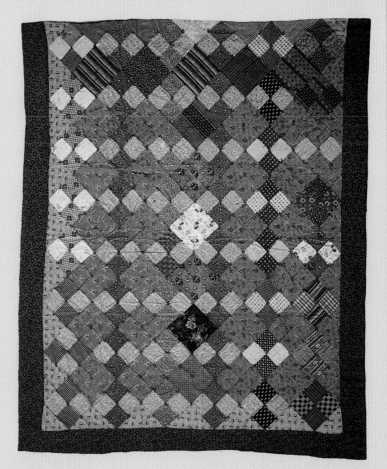

A.

B.

A Hanging Four Patch,
circa 1880, Pennsylvania,
excellent condition,
$650.00 – 750.00.

**B. Hanging Four Patches
on Point,** circa 1880,
Pennsylvania, excellent
condition, $500.00 – 600.00.

**C. One Patch on Point with
Rectangle Border,** 69" x 80",
circa 1870, New England,
excellent condition,
$600.00 – 800.00.

C.

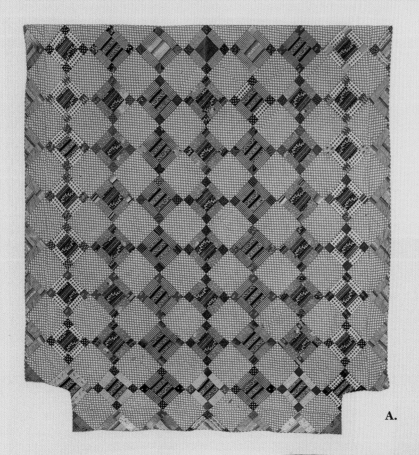

A.

B.

A. Extended Nine Patch, 72" x 76", circa 1820, quilt-maker was from the Bartlett family from Derry, Epping, and Notingham near the Piscataqua/Great Bay, Cocheaca River, New Hampshire, good variety of prints and colors including Prussian blue, note 10" cut for four-poster bed, $1,800.00 – 2,000.00.

B. Nine Patch, 72" x 78", circa 1830, quiltmaker was from the Bartlett family from Derry, Epping, and Notingham near the Piscataqua/Great Bay, Cocheaca River, New Hampshire, finding two quilts with some of the same fabrics and provenance enhances desirability, $1,800.00 – 2,000.00.

A. Extended Nine Patch or Puss in the Corner, 102" x 102", circa 1800, Vermont, great quilt for the study of the early fabrics including blue resist, red resist, and chintz in several colors, the backing is linen and the four-poster cutout is 21", rare, $1,800.00 – 2,000.00.

B. Nine Patch, 85" x 96", circa 1865, Indiana, quilts made in the years surrounding the Civil War are of great interest to many collectors, $700.00 – 900.00.

C. Nine Patch Chain, 78" x 78", circa 1875, Pennsylvania, excellent condition, $600.00 – 800.00.

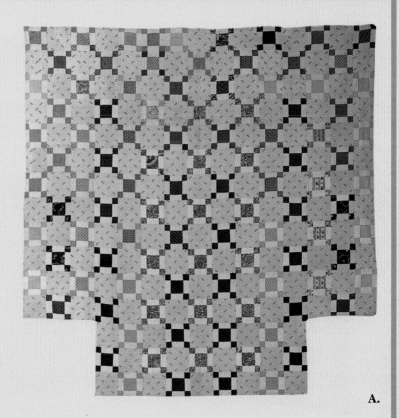

A.

B.

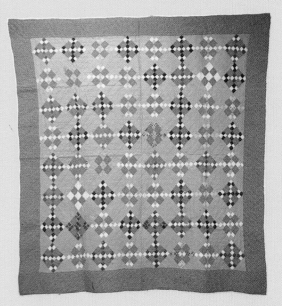

C.

A.

A. Uneven Nine Patch Center Medallion, 110" x 110", circa 1830, Philadephia, Pennsylvania, careful arrangement of blocks form an inner frame, twill tape binding, chintz sashing, quilted in diagonal parallel lines, excellent condition, $3,500.00 – 4,500.00.

B. Four Patch Set in Nine Patches, 66" x 72", circa 1900, Pennsylvania, excellent condition, $500.00 – 700.00.

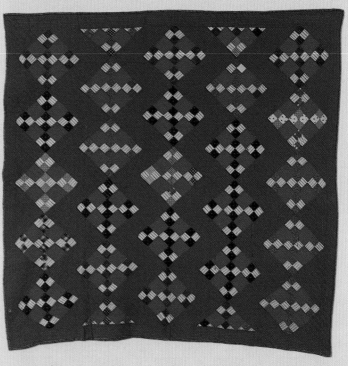

B.

A.

A. Nine Patch, 78" x 81",
1924, Monroe, Ohio, made for
the daughter of Mabel (Ashley)
Kettman from her baby
dresses, by Mabel's mother,
dated November 1924, a good
example of scrap quilts made
in the first quarter of the
twentieth century,
$600.00 – 800.00.

B. Hanging Nine Patch,
78" x 78", circa 1880, Adams
County, Pennsylvania,
$400.00 – 600.00.

B.

A.

B.

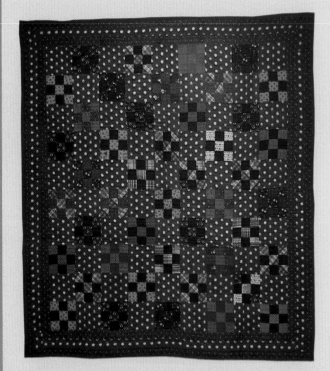

C.

A. Nine in Nine, 80" x 82",
circa 1890, Zigzag setting,
very good condition,
$600.00 – 700.00.

B. Churn Dash Variation,
62" x 76", circa 1890,
Indiana, excellent
condition, $500.00 – 700.00.

C. Nine Patch, 75" x 85",
circa 1880, Pennsylvania,
wool, excellent condition,
$700.00 – 900.00.

A.

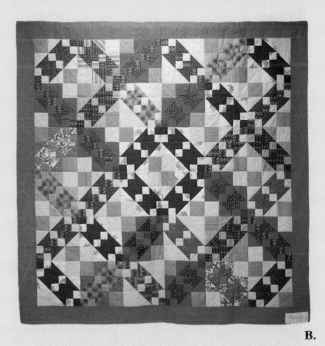

B.

A. Jacob's Ladder, circa 1910, Midwest, excellent condition, $500.00 – 600.00.

B. Anvil and Four Patch, 82" x 84", circa 1890, Lancaster County, Pennsylvania, maker was Naomi Landis, very graphic, excellent condition, $800.00 – 1,000.00.

C. Four Patch Economy Block Set on Point, circa 1880, Pennsylvania, excellent condition, $650.00 – 750.00.

C.

A.

A. Economy Patch, 83" x 96", circa 1820, Massachusetts, Clamshell quilting, excellent workmanship, excellent condition, $2,400.00 – 2,600.00.

B. Economy Patch, circa 1880, Pennsylvania, excellent condition, $1,400.00 – 1,600.00.

C. Album or Friendship Block, 94" x 94", circa 1840, Philadelphia, Pennsylvania, no signatures, excellent condition, $2,400.00 – 2,600.00.

B.

C.

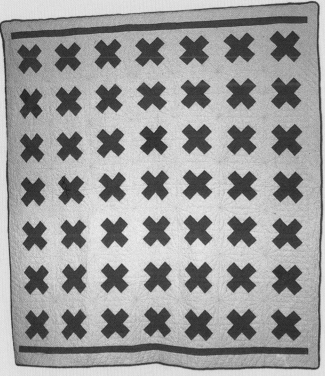

B.

A.

C.

A. String Pieced Lattice,
67" x 77", circa 1950,
Tennessee, initialed,
$300.00 – 500.00.

B. Red Cross Quilt,
72" x 76", circa 1917, red and
white top and bottom
borders, heavily quilted,
excellent condition,
$700.00 – 900.00.

C. Red Cross Quilt,
83" x 94", circa 1917,
excellent condition,
$800.00 – 1,000.00.

A.

B.

C.

A. Pinwheel Pattern, 74" x 85", 1942, nylon, Midwest, excellent workmanship, excellent condition, $500.00 – 600.00.

B. Roman Cross, 80" x 80", circa 1890, Indiana, $500.00 – 700.00.

C. Double Crosses, circa 1880, Pennsylvania, unusual on navy blue, pink inner border, excellent condition, $700.00 – 900.00.

A.

B.

A. Album, 75" x 79", signed
on two blocks in ink, "April
1847" and "1847," Hamburgh,
New York, excellent
condition, $900.00 – 1,200.00.

B. Nine Patch, 56" x 82",
circa 1910, made in Quebec,
Canada, by Catholic nuns,
$400.00 – 600.00.

C. Irish Chain, 70" x 84",
circa 1920, Iowa,
$800.00 – 1,000.00.

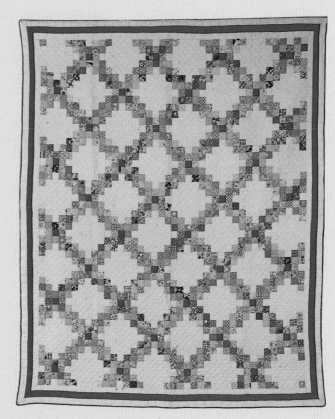

C.

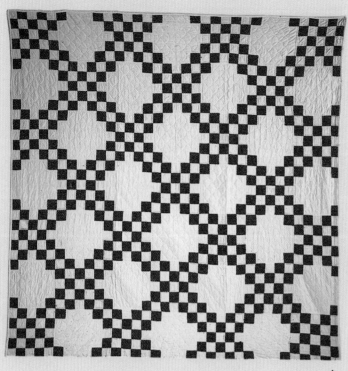

A.

B.

A. Single Irish Chain, circa 1860, New England, excellent condition, $400.00 – 500.00.

B. The Peaceful Valley Quilt, 70" x 85", dated in the quilting, 1877, fair/good condition, heavily quilted, $600.00 – 800.00.

C. Double Irish Chain, circa 1860, Ohio, fine quilting, square on point, inner border and outer border, excellent condition, $750.00 – 850.00.

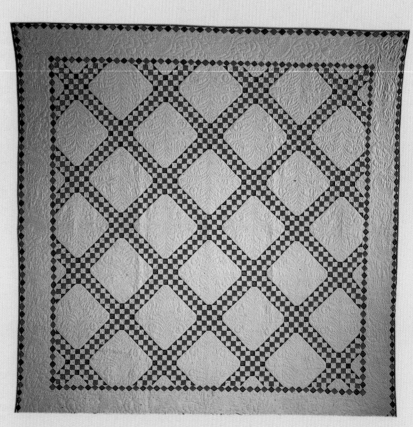

C.

A.

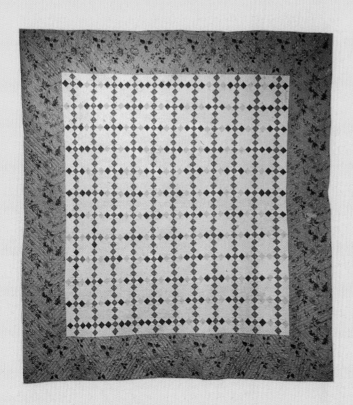

A. Irish Chain, 84" x 84", circa 1885, Ephrata, Pennsylvania, excellent condition and craftsmanship, $1,600.00 – 1,800.00.

B. Nine Patch on Point with 12" Chintz Border, 82" x 91", 1842, Analuca Stausburg 1842 in quilting, back to front edge finish, slight staining, heavily quilted, $3,000.00 – 3,500.00.

B.

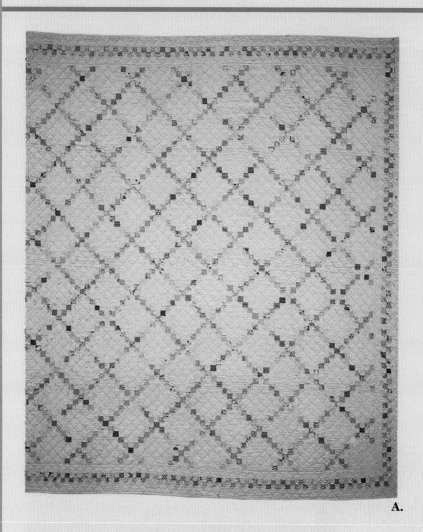

A.

A. Crisscross, 73" x 80", circa 1930, Indiana, made from a newspaper pattern by Nancy Page, excellent condition, $800.00 – 1,000.00.

B. Mosaic #17, 82" x 86", circa 1870, New England, excellent condition, $300.00 – 500.00.

C. Mosaic #17, 75" x 78", circa 1900, made in Iowa, excellent condition, $900.00 – 1,100.00.

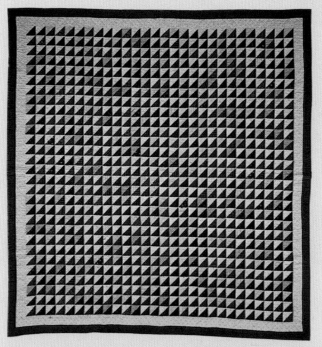

C.

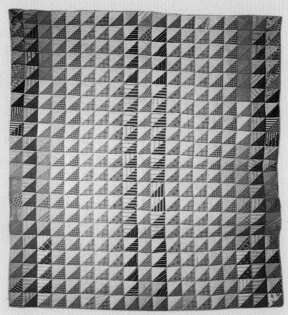

B.

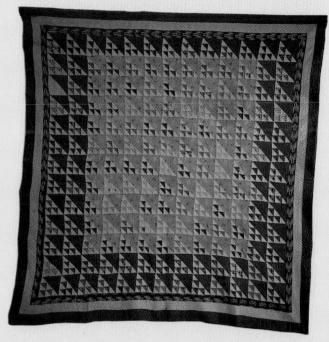

A.

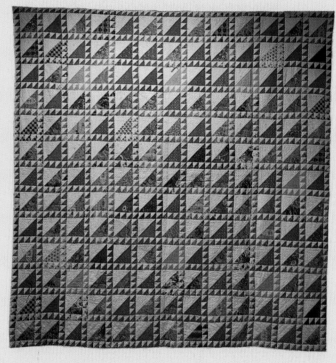

B.

A. Wild Goose Chase Medallion,
circa 1860, New England, excellent
condition, $750.00 – 850.00.

B. Lady of the Lake, 92" x 92",
circa 1840, New England, excellent
workmanship, excellent condition,
$2,800.00 – 3,000.00.

C. Birds in the Air, 99" x 99",
circa 1830, New York, heavily
quilted, $2,500.00 – 3,000.00.

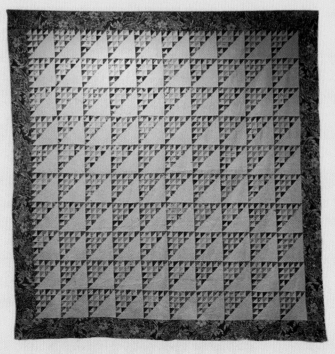

C.

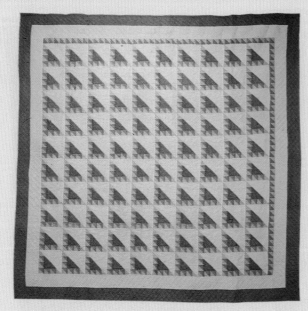

A.

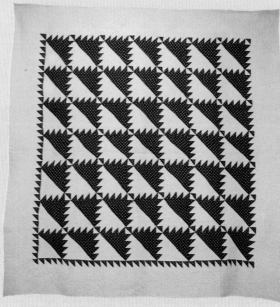

B.

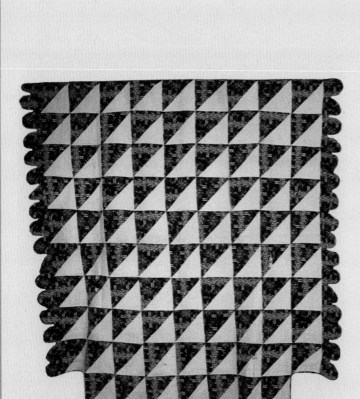

C.

A. Delectable Mountain,
84" x 84", circa 1880, Berks
County, Pennsylvania,
arranged in diagonal set, a
lot of color activity as colors
used are of the same
intensity, $800.00 – 900.00.

**B. Delectable Mountains
Set Diagonal,** circa 1860,
Vermont, indigo and white is
the most popular, two-color
combination in quilts, very
graphic, unusual set,
excellent condition,
$1,200.00 – 1,500.00.

C. Half-square Triangles,
72" x 78", circa 1845,
Virginia, blue, red, and
unbleached muslin, unusual
scallops as border treatment,
few small stains,
$700.00 – 900.00.

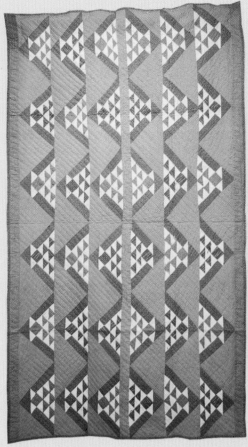

A.

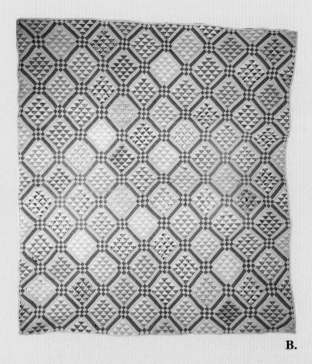

B.

A. Baskets (no handles),
circa 1880, New England,
baskets form zigzag pattern,
Hired Hand's quilt or Hired
Man's quilt, $650.00 – 750.00.

B. Birds in the Air,
73" x 84", circa 1870, New
Hampshire, very unusual set,
excellent condition,
$800.00 – 1,000.00.

C. Lady of the Lake,
76" x 76", circa 1875,
Vermont,
$1,100.00 – 1,300.00.

C.

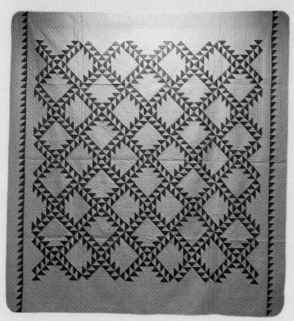

A.

B.

C.

A. Lady of the Lake, 84" x 88", circa 1910, Massachusetts, beautifully pieced, quilted, and designed, blue and white with Sawtooth borders on two sides, excellent condition, one of four quilts from the Proudfit family, $1,800.00 – 2,000.00.

B. Ocean Waves Variation, 84" x 84", 1885, Massachusetts, signed "Mary Proudfit," excellent workmanship, excellent condition, $1,800.00 – 2,000.00.

C. Ocean Waves with Zig-zag Border, 71" x 80", circa 1890, Berks County, Pennsylvania, printed fabric in alternate blocks adds dimension, excellent work-manship, excellent condition, $900.00 – 1,100.00.

A. Ocean Wave, 76" x 79",
circa 1910, made in Indiana,
excellent condition,
$700.00 – 900.00.

B. Ocean Waves, 92" x 96",
circa 1860, Pennsylvania, a
great example of the graphic
abilities of this pattern when
the pattern is used on color
(dark green) inner frame,
border, etc, excellent
condition,
$2,600.00 – 2,800.00.

C. Ocean Waves, 82" x 84",
circa 1895, Pennsylvania,
very unusual set, red and
green pinwheels form cen-
ters where waves intersect,
wave yellow against purple,
borders of green, purple, and
red, very graphic and very
unusual, excellent
condition,
$1,200.00 – 1,400.00.

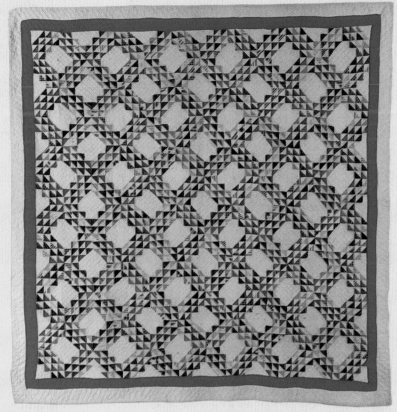

A.

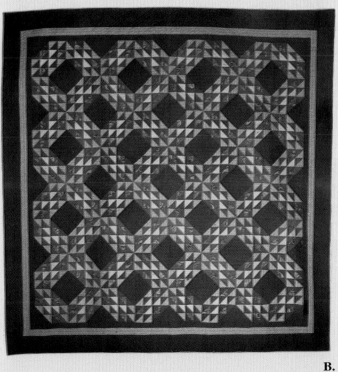

B.

C.

A.

C.

B.

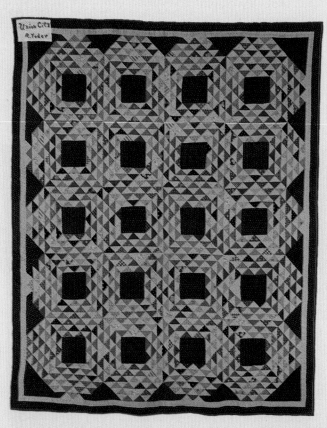

D.

A. Ocean Waves on Red with Borders, 79" x 82", circa 1885, very unusual and very graphic, excellent condition, $1,100.00 – 1,300.00.

B. Ocean Waves Variation, 74" x 93", circa 1890, Pennsylvania, excellent condition, $900.00 – 1,100.00.

C. Ocean Waves, 92" x 94", circa 1870, Pennsylvania, some fading, heavily quilted, applied binding, $2,600.00 – 2,800.00.

D. Ocean Wave, 76" x 96", circa 1880, labeled "Union City, R. Yoder," made in Pennsylvania, $1,500.00 – 1,700.00.

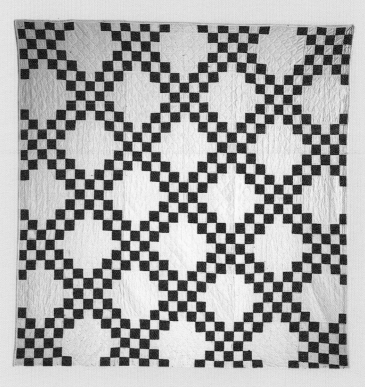

A.

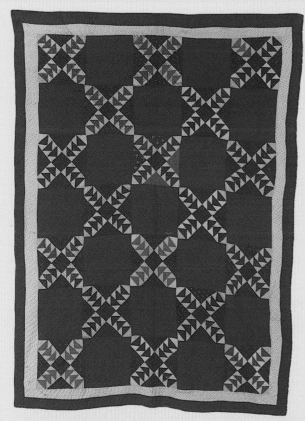

B.

C.

A. Irish Chain, 1860, New England, excellent condition, $400.00 – 500.00.

B. Wild Goose Chase, 68" x 92", circa 1890, Kentucky, $500.00 – 700.00.

C, Wild Goose Chase, 73" x 81", Ohio, 1867, written in quilting, "Our Father Who Art in Heaven, Christian A. Fisher, 1867," $1,500.00 – 1,700.00.

A.

B.

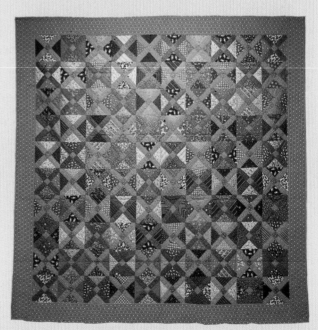

C.

A. Wild Goose Chase,
84" x 99", circa 1860,
Vermont, some fading of
purple, $600.00 – 700.00.

B. Four "T" Block on Point,
78" x 90", circa 1840, Ohio,
excellent condition,
$1,800.00 – 2,000.00.

C. Italian Tile, 82" x 88",
circa 1895, Pennsylvania,
great graphics, excellent
condition, $700.00 – 900.00.

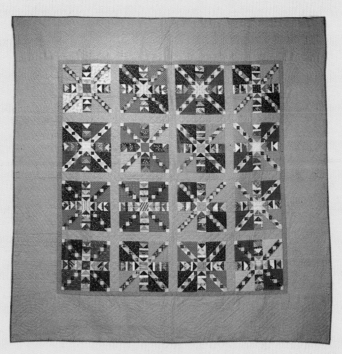

A.

A. Wild Goose Chase Variation, 84" x 84", circa 1900, Pennsylvania, very graphic, excellent workmanship, excellent condition, $1,000.00 – 1,200.00.

B. Wagon Wheel or Fireworks, 68" x 74", 1890, made by Emma M. Faust Maugans of rural Peru, Indiana, documented a blue ribbon winner in the Indiana State Fair, $800.00 – 1,000.00.

B.

A.

B.

C.

A. Railroad Crossing, 80" x 80", signed "Mother, Clara, 1936," Indiana, rare, $1,700.00 – 1,900.00.

B. Single Wedding Ring, 80" x 80", circa 1890, made in Indiana, the backing of this quilt is a large piece of mourning print, the woven tape edge finish is unusual for this time period, $500.00 – 700.00.

C. Sashed Four Block, 60" x 66", circa 1870, Pennsylvania, diagonal line quilting, excellent condition, $900.00 – 1,100.00.

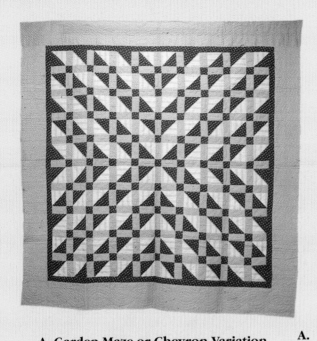

A.

B.

A. Garden Maze or Chevron Variation, 73" x 74", circa 1885, front to back edge finish, red and blue bars on back, excellent condition, $800.00 – 1,000.00.

B. Split Nine Patch, 75" x 75", circa 1935, Perkioman Valley, Pennsylvania, Barn Raising set, $600.00 – 800.00.

C. Split Nine Patch, 80" x 82", circa 1890, Perkioman Valley, Pennsylvania, excellent condition, $1,000.00 – 1,200.00.

D. Split Nine Patch, 81" x 82", circa 1910, Perkioman Valley, Pennsylvania, excellent condition, $1,000.00 – 1,200.00.

C.

D.

113

A.

B.

C.

A. Split Nine Patch,
84" x 88", 1940, Perkioman
Valley, Pennsylvania, set in a
Barn Raising on point,
excellent condition,
$1,000.00 – 1,200.00.

B. Split Nine Patch,
79" x 82", circa 1940,
Perkioman Valley,
Pennsylvania, very unusual
and very graphic,
excellent condition,
$1,100.00 – 1,300.00.

**C. Split Nine Patch
Variation,** 78" x 78", circa
1910, Perkioman Valley,
Pennsylvania, excellent
condition, $600.00 – 800.00.

A.

B.

C.

A. One Patch, 77" x 90", circa 1880, Pennsylvania, arranged in contrasting rows arranged diagonally, great visuals, excellent condition, $700.00 – 900.00.

B. Trip around the World, 68" x 84", circa 1930, Kansas, $400.00 – 600.00.

C. Center Medallion, 81" x 86", circa 1880, George Washington Centennial fabric in center, excellent condition, $1,000.00 – 1,200.00.

115

A.

B.

C.

A. Trip Around the World,
81" x 81", circa 1890,
Pennsylvania, excellent
condition, $1,300.00 – 1,500.00.

B. Trip around the World,
79" x 80", circa 1880, Lancaster
County, Pennsylvania, excellent
condition, $1,800.00 – 2,000.00.

C. Philadelphia Pavement, 74"
x 88", circa 1930, Iowa, $700.00
– 800.00.

A. Hexagon Mosaic, ink stamp, "1851 EC," 83" x 95", chintz border, moderately quilted, knife edge finish, excellent condition, $1,700.00 – 1,900.00.

B. Octagon Snowball Variation, 80" x 90", circa 1875, excellent condition, $600.00 – 750.00.

C. Four Patch, 68" x 72", 1905, made in Royal Center, Indiana, by Eunice Amanda Descans Hicks, excellent condition, graphic, $300.00 – 500.00.

A.

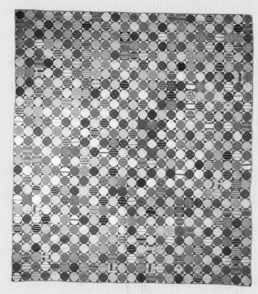

B.

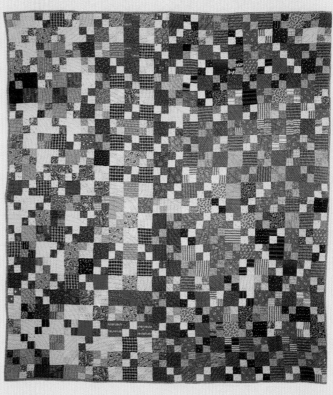

C.

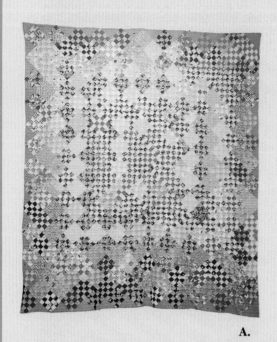

A.

B.

A. Sixteen Patch Center Medallion, 65" x 73", circa 1910, Arkansas, excellent condition, $600.00 – 800.00.

B. Nine Patch, each patch contains 16 pieces, 77" x 75", circa 1885, Massachusetts, made of 11,664 – ½" squares, rare, excellent condition, $2,600.00 – 2,800.00.

C. Postage Stamp, 79" x 88", 1892, Bucyrus, Ohio, dated 1892, 5,076 pieces, excellent condition, $1,500.00 – 1,700.00.

C.

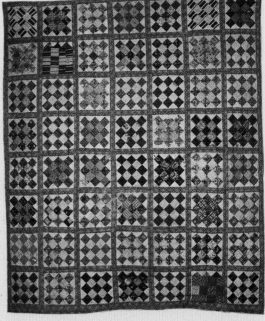

A.

B.

A. Postage Stamp, circa 1940, Iowa, set in Sunshine and Shadow arrangement, excellent workmanship, excellent condition, 2,500.00.

B. Hanging Nine Patch, 90" x 92", circa 1850, Pennsylvania, excellent condition, $2,800.00 – 3,000.00.

C. **Grandmother's Prize Chintz Sampler,** 71" x 82, circa 1840, good condition, restoration in three blocks done about 1870, $1,000.00 – 1,200.00.

C.

119

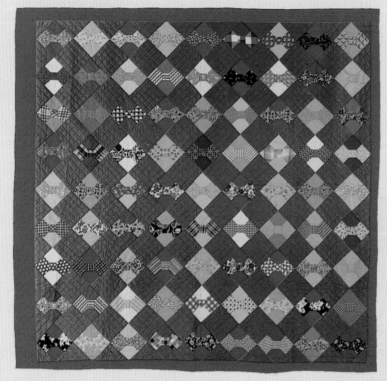

A.

B.

C.

A. Bow Tie, 76" x 76", circa 1940, made in Texas, $500.00 – 700.00.

B. Bear Paw, circa 1880, Midwest, excellent condition, $600.00 – 700.00.

C. Broken Dishes Variation, circa 1880, New England, excellent condition, excellent workmanship, $1,000.00 – 1,200.00.

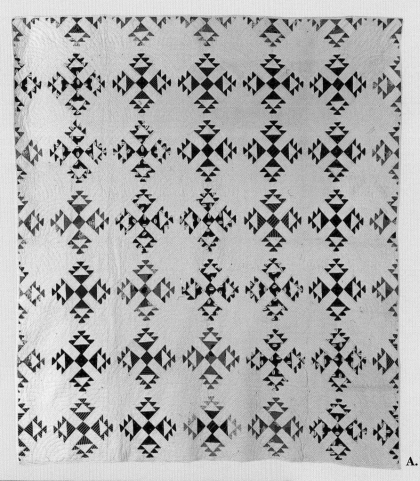

A.

A. Four Baskets, 74" x 78",
circa 1900, Indiana,
$800.00 – 1,000.00.

B. Single Wedding Ring,
64" x 80", circa 1900,
Indiana, excellent condition,
$800.00 – 1,000.00.

B.

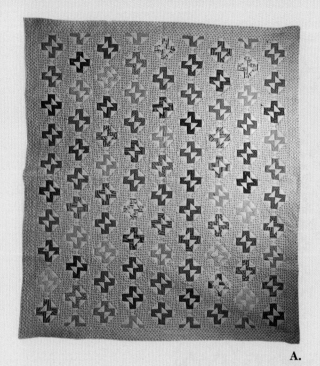

A.

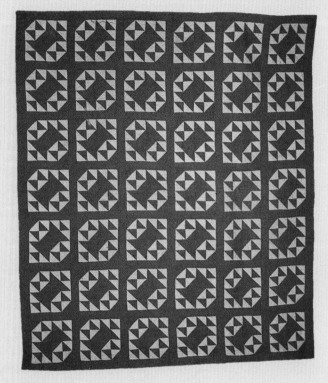

B.

C.

A. Brown Goose, 79" x 88", circa 1850, New Hampshire, signed, "Mary E. Higgins." excellent condition, $450.00 – 600.00.

B. Crosses and Losses, 71" x 80", circa 1880, excellent workmanship, excellent condition, $400.00 – 600.00.

C. Bars and Stars, 70" x 82", circa 1918, Indiana, excellent condition, from New Waterwheel pattern published by Nancy Cabot, $700.00 – 900.00.

A.

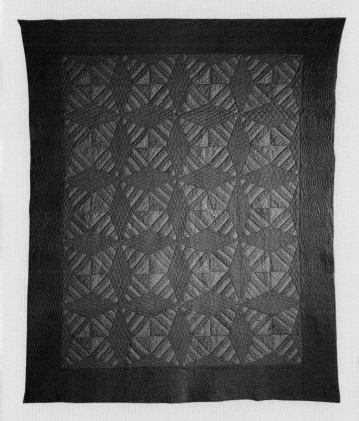

B.

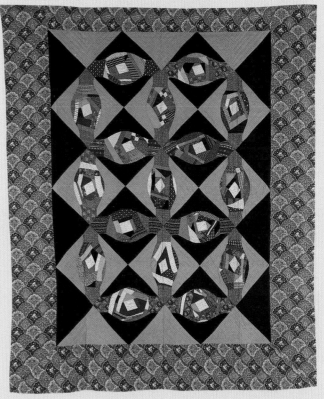

C.

A. Orange Peel (string pieced) Variation, 80" x 80", circa 1865, Zigzag border, $1,200.00 – 1,400.00

B. Rocky Road to Kansas, circa 1930, Pennsylvania, excellent condition, $550.00 – 650.00.

C. Original Design Quilt, 79" x 93", 1880, Pennsylvania, a crazy patch in a geometric set on point, paisley border, excellent workmanship, excellent condition, unusual, note the preprinted Clamshell patchwork fabric in the border, $750.00 – 1,000.00.

A.

B.

C.

A. Rocky Road to California, 76" x 78", circa 1890, Pennsylvania, excellent condition, $600.00 – 800.00.

B. London Road, 78" x 86", circa 1890, Pennsylvania, excellent condition, $1,200.00 – 1,400.00.

C. Pieced Tulip, 68" x 90", circa 1880, North Carolina, Nine Patch posts, good allover quilting, excellent condition, $400.00 – 600.00.

A.

B.

A. King David's Crown,
75" x 86", circa 1845, New
York, good condition,
$900.00 – 1,100.00.

B. Caesar's Crown,
99" x 99", circa 1830,
Vermont, excellent condition,
$2,600.00 – 2,800.00.

C. Improved Nine Patch,
65" x 72", circa 1930,
Midwest, yellow background,
excellent condition,
$400.00 – 600.00.

C.

A.

B.

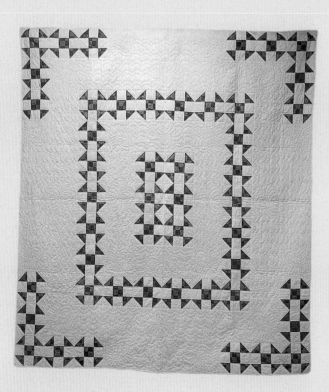

C.

A. Cobweb Variation,
68" x 81", circa 1950, Midwest, visually exciting use of
large print in negative areas,
$400.00 – 600.00.

B. Nosegay, 70" x 85", circa
1950, made in Arkansas,
excellent condition,
$700.00 – $900.00.

C. Shoofly Medallion,
73" x 83", circa 1960,
Missouri, excellent condition,
$400.00 – 600.00.

A.

A. Trip around the World,
77" x 86", circa 1940, Barry
County, Michigan, made by
Elizabeth Douglas, squares
are 1", excellent condition,
$600.00 – 800.00.

B. Triple Triangles,
70" x 74", circa 1890, from
the Jenkins family of
Williamsburg, Kentucky,
$650.00 – 850.00.

B.

127

A.

B.

C.

A. Drunkard's Path, 63" x 79", 1884, Massachusetts, $600.00 – 800.00.

B. Double Pinwheel, 72" x 72", circa 1940, Pennsylvania, very graphic, excellent condition, $700.00 – 900.00.

C. Queen's Crown with Pieced Corner Posts, 77" x 90", circa 1910, Pennsylvania, excellent condition, $1,200.00 – 1,400.00.

A. Economy Patch Center Medallion, 88" x 100", circa 1820, Pennsylvania, $2,400.00 – 2,600.00.

B. Sampler Quilt with Off-set Center Medallion, 66" x 77", circa 1920, moderately quilted, excellent condition, $700.00 – 900.00.

C. Sampler Quilt, 80" x 80", circa 1890, Texas, unusual design, excellent condition, $600.00 – 800.00.

A.

B.

C.

A.

B.

C.

A. Sampler Quilt, 76" x 82",
1940, Indiana,
$600.00 – 800.00.

B. Sampler Quilt,
64"x 80", circa 1895,
moderately quilted, very
good condition,
$450.00 – 550.00.

C. Sampler, 85" x 85", 1940,
made by Jessie Levengood
in Pennsylvania,
excellent workmanship,
excellent condition,
$1,400.00 – 1,600.00.

A.

B.

A. Wool Comfort – String Spider Web Blocks, excellent condition, $600.00 – 800.00.

B. Sampler Quilt, 70" x 76", circa 1890, made in Pennsylvania by members of the Miller family, $1,400.00 – 1,600.00.

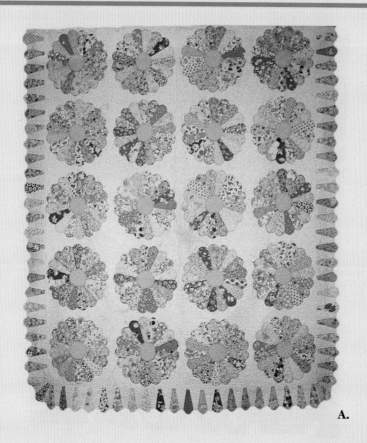

A.

A. Dresden Plate with Ice Cream Border, 72" x 83", circa 1930, handquilted, very good condition, $500.00 – 600.00.

B. Unusual Pattern, 81" x 92", circa 1950, excellent condition, graphic, $700.00 – 900.00.

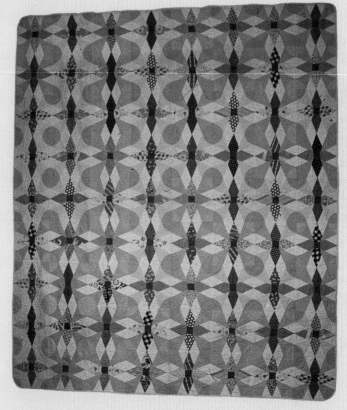

B.

Preprinted Patchwork, 76" x 82", circa 1880, often found as a backing, "cheater" cloth was a popular fabric in the second half of the nineteenth century although it debuted much earlier, $500.00 – 700.00.

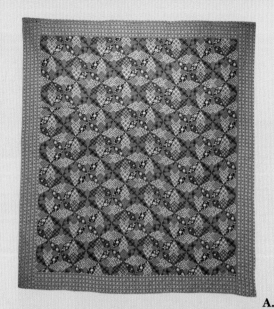

A.

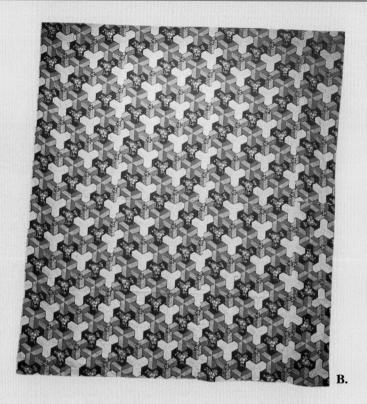

B.

C.

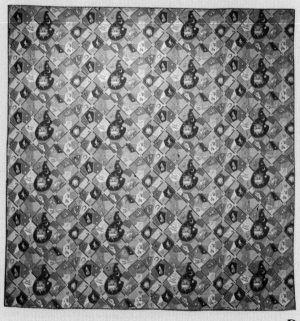

D.

A. Preprinted Patchwork,
73" x 83", circa 1890, Pennsylvania,
$400.00 – 600.00.

B. Pre-printed Patchwork,
81" x 91", circa 1890, front to back
edge finish, excellent condition,
$400.00 – 600.00.

C. Preprinted Patchwork,
94" x 101", circa 1875, Pennsylvania,
centennial fabric, excellent condition,
$400.00 – 600.00.

D. Preprinted Patchwork,
96" x 96", circa 1885, Pennsylvania,
excellent condition, $400.00 – 600.00.

A.

B.

A. Preprinted Patchwork,
73" x 89", circa 1830, New
England, chintz cheater
cloth with printed stripe
borders and backing, rare,
excellent condition,
$1,200.00 – 1,500.00.

B. Preprinted Patchwork,
72" x 82", circa 1875, New
England, excellent condition,
$300.00 – 500.00.

**C. Four Block in Bars
Center Medallion,**
66" x 77", circa 1880, New
England, bars are surrounded
by preprinted patchwork cut
into large triangles and
pieced into a Sawtooth
border, $800.00 – 1,000.00.

C.

Crazy Quilt, 70 x 70", circa 1895, made by Hattie P. Dyer, Boston, Massachusetts, a milliner who sewed her label into the quilt, velvets, heavily embroidered, excellent condition, unusual border, $5,800.00 – 6,000.00.

A. Crazy Patch, 56" x 57", 1886, inscribed "G. R. /To Momma from Carrie, XMAS '86," appliqué, embroidery, ruching, painting, and French knots are combined with featherstitching, $1,000.00 – 1,200.00.

B. Crazy Quilt, 53" x 59", 1886, initialed "J .R .H. /Joe from Carrie, XMAS '86," typical quilt of the popular crazy patch fad stitched with pets and nature motifs, initials are very elaborate and the inscription and date add value, $1,200.00 – 1,500.00.

C. Crazy Quilt, 71" x 71", 1890, unusual example of the crazy quilt style, made entirely of cotton fabrics, mostly prints, fans, crosses, horseshoes, keys, and stars used are motifs found during the fourth quarter of the nineteenth century, $600.00 – 800.00.

A.

B.

C.

A. Crazy Patch, 72" x 71",
circa 1890, Pennsylvania,
wool, excellent condition,
$600.00 – 700.00.

B. Crazy Quilt, 83" x 67",
circa 1900, Oley Valley,
Pennsylvania. The large
pieces with no embroidery
are typical of the type of
crazy quilt made at the end
of the fad.
$900.00 – 1,200.00.

A.

B.

A.

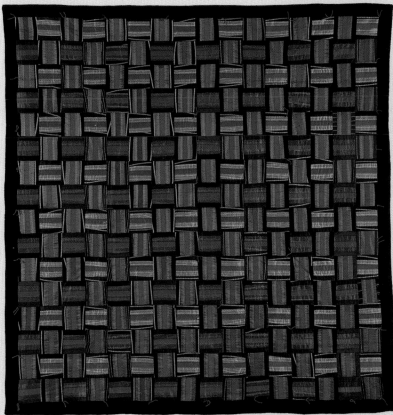

B.

A. Hexagon Mosaic,
55" x 63", circa 1875, Lincoln,
Illinois, made Rebecsa Gray,
silks and satins, English style
paper pieced.
$1,500.00 – 1,800.00.

**B. Roman Square Tied
Comfort,** 70" x 71" 1890.
Great use of striped fabric to
produce a woven effect,
$500.00 – 700.00.

139

A.

A. Mennonite Lattice Quilt,
78" x 79", circa 1890, Lebanon County, Pennsylvania, embroidery along seams, black fabric used for setting the wool, silk, and satin fabrics is highlighted by the embroidery, excellent workmanship, excellent condition.
$800.00 – 1,100.00.

B. Mennonite Indian Hatchet,
79" x 79", circa 1900, Pennsylvania, wool with embroidered fancy stitching along seams, very graphic, excellent condition,
$600.00 – 800.00.

C. Fans, 74" x 75", circa 1910, Pennsylvania, wool, embroidered edges of fans,
$600.00 – 800.00.

B.

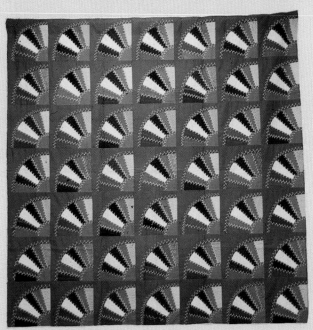

C.

A.

B.

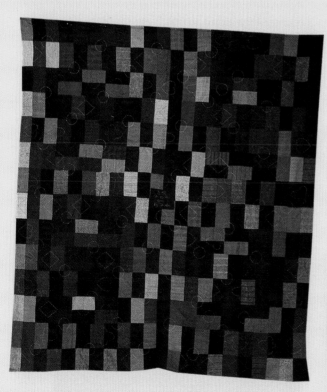

C.

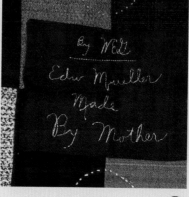

D.

A. Center Medallion, 78" x 90", circa 1890, Pennsylvania, wool, economy patches and squares surrounding central embroidered element, embroidery on squares, $900.00 – 1,100.00.

B. Detail of center embroidered element.

C. One Patch, 72" x 82", circa 1900, Illinois, wool, signed "WEG – Edw. Mueller – Made by Mother," excellent condition, $650.00 – 750.00.

D. Detail of One Patch, quilted with diamonds, circle, clubs, and heart designs.

A.

B.

A. Crazy Quilt, 70" x 82", circa 1900, Pennsylvania, wool, excellent condition, $500.00 – 600.00.

B. Zigzag Bricks, 74" x 74", circa 1900, Pennsylvania, wool with multicolored embroidery along seams, very graphic, $800.00 – 900.00.

C. Touching Stars, 57" x 57", circa 1900, Pennsylvania, wool, embroidered seams and felted wool outer border with fancy cut decorative edge, excellent workmanship, excellent condition, $800.00 – 900.00.

D. Detail of Touching Stars.

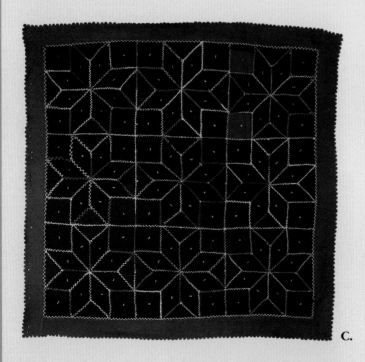

C.

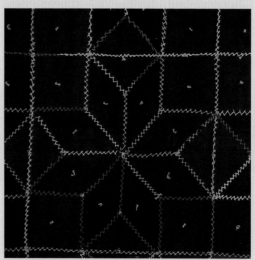

D.

Rare or Unusual Examples

A.

B.

A. Quaker Medallion,
96" x 96", circa 1810,
Philadelphia, Pennsylvania,
pieced, appliquéd, ribbon
embroidery, embroidery,
linen, cotton, and silk, some
fading and some wear,
$900.00 – 1,000.00.

B. Whole Cloth Chintz,
66" x 83", circa 1820, New
England, four poster cut-out,
some fading,
$200.00 – 400.00.

A.

A. Early Copperplate or Early Roller Mono-chromes, circa 1790 – 1810, linen back, moderately quilted, excellent condition, $1,600.00 – 1,800.00.

B. Grid of Lattice, 109" x 112", circa 1820, New England, linen back, signed, "Annie Tommals," excellent condition, rare, $3,000.00 – 3,500.00.

C. Detail of Grid of Lattice.

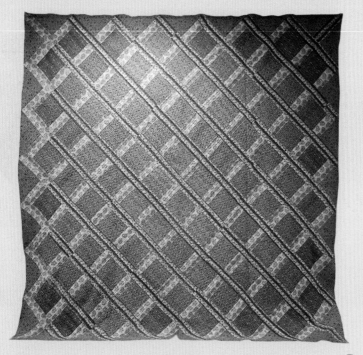

B.

C.

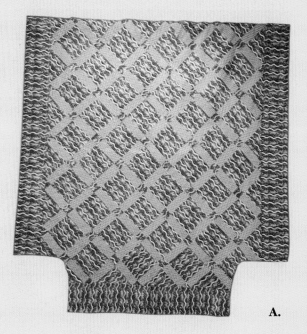

A.

B.

A. Lattice Squares, circa 1830, Massachusetts, wool challis, $1,600.00 – 1,800.00.

B. Compass, 77" x 79", circa 1840, New England, compass is light set against darker ombre plaid stripe with a Sawtooth border and stars at each juncture, very graphic, unusual/rare, excellent condition, $2,800.00 – 3,000.00.

C. Sunflower, 87" x 87", circa 1840, North Carolina, beautifully quilted and very graphic, blue, red, and yellow on light, excellent condition, $2,400.00 – 2,600.00.

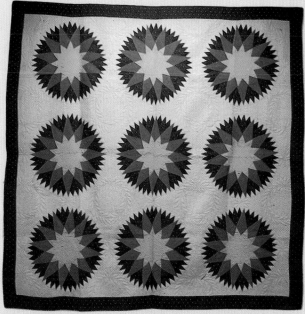

C.

A.

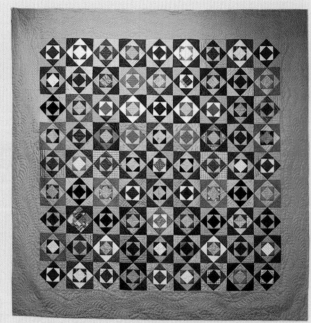

B.

C.

A. Medallion Starburst, 72" x 80", circa 1860, Pennsylvania, made in bold colors and dramatic patchwork quite often found in appliqué, colors are without fading, quilting very good and the condition excellent, $1,800.00 – 2,000.00.

B. Shadow Box, 88" x 88", circa 1850, Philadelphia, Quaker, silk, beautifully and heavily quilted, woven tape binding, excellent condition, rare, $3,800.00.

C. Shadows, 81" x 92", circa 1870, Ephrata, Pennsylvania, hearts quilted-in pieced border, sampler of quilting designs, excellent condition, $2,600.00 – 2,800.00.

A.

B.

C.

A. Field of Diamonds,
76" x 89", circa 1860, wool
challis, English paper pieced,
whole cloth solid chintz
(glazed backing), excellent
workmanship, excellent
condition, rare extraordinary,
$3,300.00 – 3,500.00.

**B. Hexagon Mosiac with
Zigzag Borders,** 81" x 84",
circa 1850, hand quilted, fair
condition, $800.00 – 1,000.00.

C. Houses, 70" x 88",
circa 1930, New England,
excellent workmanship,
excellent condition,
$1,000.00 – 1,200.00.

A.

B.

A. **Mennonite Sawtooth Diamond,** 76" x 76", circa 1885, Lancaster County, Pennsylvania, excellent quilting, excellent condition, $2,800.00 – 3,000.00.

B. **Sawtooth Diamond,** 75" x 77", circa 1870, Landis family, Lancaster, County, Pennsylvania, excellent workmanship, excellent condition, $2,200.00 – 2,400.00.

C. **Carpenter's Square,** 90" x 90", circa 1880, Pennsylvania, excellent workmanship, excellent condition, $1,500.00 – 1,700.00.

C.

A. Pine Tree, 77" x 80", circa 1875, excellent workmanship, excellent condition, $2,800.00 – 3,000.00.

B. Cake Stand, 80" x 92", circa 1940, New York, fine cotton sateen fabric, extraordinary workmanship, excellent condition, $1,200.00 – 1,400.00.

C. Detail of Cake Stand.

A.

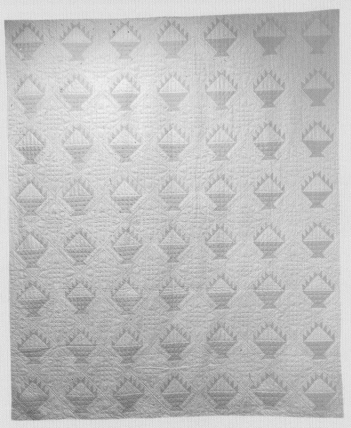

B.

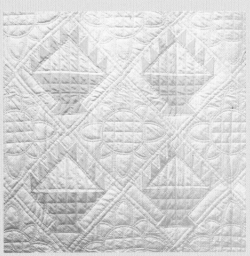

C.

149

A.

B.

A. Butterflies, 72" x 82", circa 1939, Missouri, won first prize at the 1939 Missouri State Fair, excellent condition, $600.00 – 800.00.

B. Butterfly (Moth), circa 1940, Midwest, Nine Patch corner blocks in outer borders, very unusual color and fabric use for this period, good quilting, excellent condition, $650.00 – 750.00.

C. Sunbonnet Sue, circa 1940, Midwest, unusual set, detail included, excellent condition, $400.00 – 500.00.

D. Detail of Sunbonnet Sue.

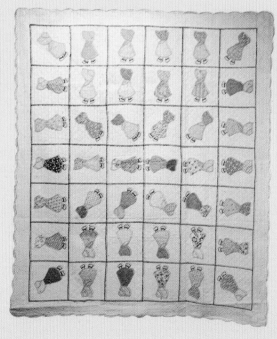

C.

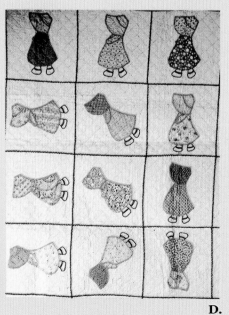

D.

A.

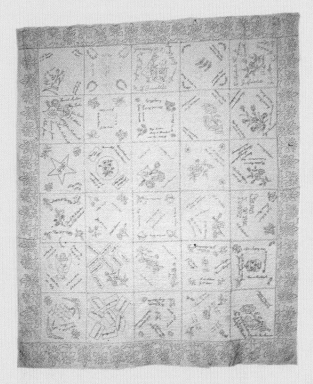

B.

A. Embroidered Baskets,
87" x 87", circa 1940,
excellent condition,
$300.00 – 500.00.

**B. Redwork Embroidered
Quilt,** 64" x 75", circa 1890,
good condition, $500.00 –
700.00.

C. Stencil Quilt, 76½" x 76½",
circa 1870, 16 blocks,
rare and unusual,
excellent condition,
$1,400.00 – 1,600.00.

C.

A.

A. Coffin Cover, Order of Odd Fellows, 42" x 72", circa 1890, Vermont, wool, silk, embroidered and embellished appliqué, very rare, $10,000.00.

B. Royal Hawaiian Flag Quilt, 80" x 80", circa 1900, standard bearers wear embroidered feather cloaks, excellent condition, $15,000.00.

C. Detail of Royal Hawaiian Flag Quilt.

B.

C.

A.

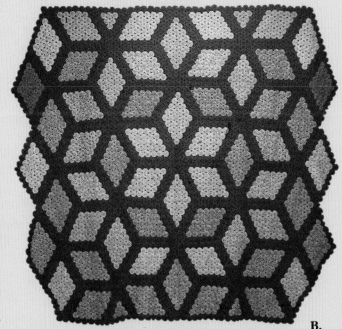

B.

A. Flag Summer Coverlet,
80" x 74", circa 1940,
made in the Midwest,
excellent condition,
$2,400.00 – 2,600.00.

B. Yoyo Coverlet, circa
1930, New Hampshire, very
graphic, purchased with a
grocery bag of completed
yoyo diamonds,
$125.00 – 175.00.

C. Chair Seat,
16" x 16", and back,
15" x 31", circa 1910, made
by Amish quiltmaker in
Ohio, household decorating
items are rare,
$75.00 – $150.00,
$100.00 – $200.00
respectively.

D. Chair back.

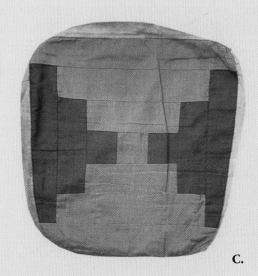

C.

D.

A.

A. Signature Album,
74" x 82", dated 1871, Maine,
names are in ink, as is the
date, finished as a summer
spread, $3,000.00 – 3,200.00.

B. Fair Play, 81" x 83", circa
1890, Pennsylvania, graphic
curved pieced design,
excellent condition,
$600.00 – 800.00.

B.

A.

A. Carolina Lily Medallion with Oak Leaf and Reel, 39" x 39", circa 1840, Lancaster, Pennsylvania, excellent workmanship, excellent condition, $3,400.00 – 3,600.00.

B. Lone Star with Nine Patch, Birds in Air, and Flying Geese Border, 46" x 46", circa 1840, Philadelphia, Pennsylvania, signed Mary M, Ellis, very unusual crib quilt, fading, some fabric loss and wear, $600.00 – 800.00.

B.

A.

B.

C.

A. Mennonite Tumbling Blocks, 53" x 59", circa 1910, Pennsylvania, excellent condition, $1,800.00 – 2,000.00.

B. Crib Quilt – "Henry Clay," 35" x 44", 1844, New York/New Jersey, Laythrop family, silk, excellent condition, $3,500.00 – 4,000.00.

C. Fragmented Blocks Child's Quilt, 39" x 41", circa 1890, made in Maine, size is a good clue to a child's quilt, patterns usually made in proportion to the size of the quilt, really unusual design for a child's quilt, $4,600.00 – 4,800.00.

A.

B.

A. Nine Patch Bar,
33" x 35", circa 1820, New
England, some fading,
$300.00 – 400.00.

B. Reverse.

**C. Italian Tile in Alternate
Blocks,** 36" x 42",
circa 1840, New England,
excellent workmanship,
excellent condition,
$2,200.00 – 2,400.00.

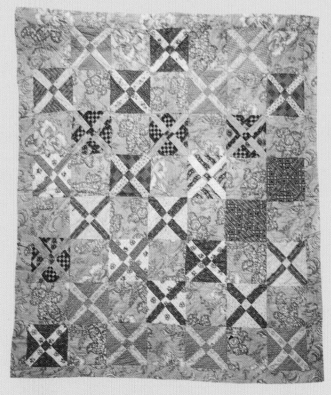

C.

157

A.

A. Fence Row, 64" x 78",
circa 1830, New York,
$700.00 – 900.00.

B. Mosaic #17, 43" x 50",
circa 1920, $500.00 – 700.00.

C. Lemoyne Star Crib Top,
39" x 39", circa 1850,
excellent condition, $225.00.

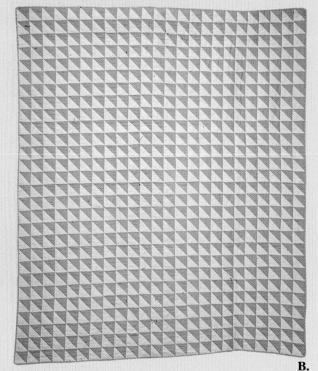

B.

C.

A.

B.

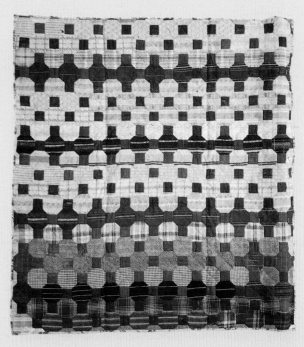

A. Four Block Appliqué Summer Spread, 39" x 39", circa 1880, Pennsylvania, $300.00 – 500.00.

B. LeMoyne Star with Flying Geese Border, 36" x 44", circa 1860, Maine, crib quilt, excellent workmanship, excellent condition, rare, $1,600.00 – 1,800.00.

C. Ozark Cobblestones, 32" x 35", circa 1830, Maine, wool, glazed chintz back and printed chintz binding, excellent condition, $600.00 – 800.00.

C.

159

A.

B.

C.

A. Nine Patch, 39" x 39",
circa 1870, $200.00 – 300.00.

B. Bricks, 25" x 35,
circa 1930, Michigan,
$500.00 – 600.00.

C. Laurel Leaf Appliqué,
35" x 45", circa 1860, New
England, Clamshell quilting
adds to the overall design,
some stains and some
thread deterioration,
$800.00 – 1,000.00.

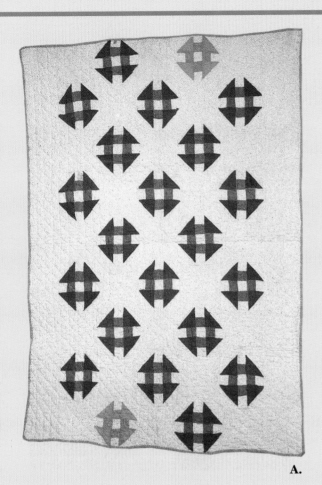

A.

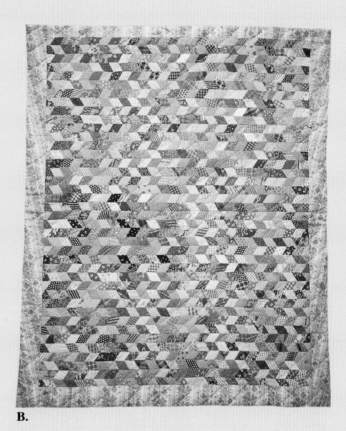

B.

A. Churn Dash Crib Quilt,
29" x 42", circa 1880,
excellent condition,
$400.00 – 500.00

B. Herringbone, 33" x 45",
circa 1850, Pennsylvania,
backing is pieced bars of
chintz fabric,
$800.00 – 1,000.00.

C. LeMoyne Star, 30" x 38",
circa 1860, made in New
England, some fading,
$300.00 – 500.00.

C.

A.

B.

C.

A. Italian Tile, 24" x 27", circa 1890, Iowa, some fading, $200.00 – 400.00.

B. Crib Quilt, 40" x 50", embroidered 1926, 1946, Prairie Point edge finish, excellent condition, $400.00 – 600.00.

C. Economy, 45" x 60", circa 1900, Pennsylvania, wool, two sided, $400.00 – 600.00.

A.

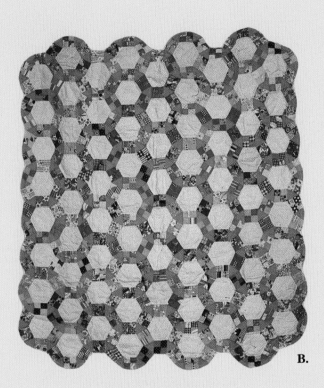

B.

C.

A. String Pieced King's X,
15" x 22", circa 1920, red
print binding, hand quilted
through each "string,"
$125.00 – 175.00.

**B. Ferris Wheel or Bride's
Bouquet,** 37" x 41", circa
1950, excellent condition,
$600.00 – 800.00.

**C. Grandmother's Flower
Garden,** 53" x 75",
circa 1930, Illinois,
excellent workmanship,
excellent condition,
$1,000.00 – 1,200.00.

A.

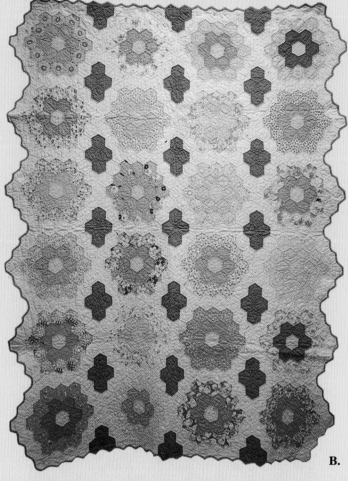

B.

C.

A. Grandmother's Flower Garden, 50" x 72", 1940, Missouri, excellent, $600.00 – 700.00.

B. Grandmother's Flower Garden Crib Quilt, 41" x 53", circa 1930, excellent condition, $550.00.

C. Stars and Flowers, 24" x 34", circa 1930, Sandwich, Ohio, colors and artistry are dramatic, $300.00 – 400.00.

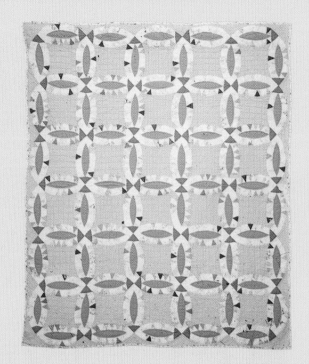

A.

B.

C.

A. Pickle Dish, 71" x 89", circa 1930, Pennsylvania, $400.00 – 600.00.

B. Embroidered Crib Quilt, circa 1930, this type of quilt was quite popular during this period, $250.00.

C. Trip around the World, 34" x 40", circa 1875, New England, $600.00 – 800.00.

A. "Baby" reversed with silk premiums, 24" x 35", circa 1920, tobacco premiums, $200.00 – 300.00.

B. Four Poster One Patch with Flounce, 12" x 12½", circa 1830, made in New England, hand embroidery on fabric for flounce is unusual in doll quilts, $300.00 – 500.00.

C. One Patch on Point, 15" x 19", circa 1860, New England, few doll quilts are made in the four-poster bed style, $200.00 – 300.00.

A.

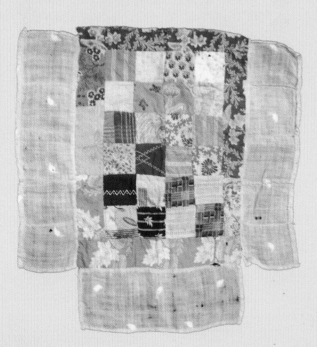

B.

C.

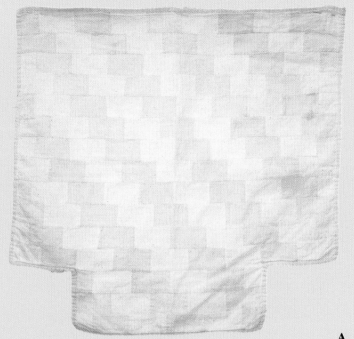

A.

B.

C.

A. Bricks Doll Quilt,
18" x 18", circa 1870,
faded, $250.00.

**B. Lemoyne Star Crib
Quilt,** 19½" x 19½", circa
1830, New England,
knife edge finish, patchwork
border, excellent condition,
$500.00 – 600.00.

C. Starburst, 19½" x 22",
circa 1910, Pennsylvania,
$150.00 – 250.00.

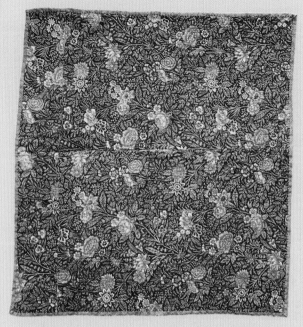

A.

B.

C.

D.

A. Doll Quilt, 17½" x 19", circa 1830, excellent condition, $175.00 – 225.00.

B. Hexagon Mosaic, circa 1830, unusual, $400.00 – 600.00.

C. Quaker Hourglass Crib Quilt, 31" x 40", circa 1850, Pennsylvania, silk, $900.00.

D. Hourglass Crib Quilt, circa 1870, rare, $700.00 – 800.00.

A.

B.

D.

C.

A. Pin Wheel, 18¼" x 18½", circa 1930,
$200.00 – 400.00.

B. Broken Dishes, 11½" x 13½", circa 1840,
Kentucky, the name "Humphries" is stamped on
this quilt, $300.00 – 500.00.

C. Alternating One Patch and Four Patches,
10" x 11½", circa 1875, $100.00 – 200.00.

D. Four Patch and Economy, 17" x 17",
circa 1890, made in New England,
$150.00 – 250.00.

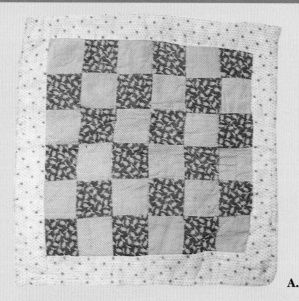

A.

B.

C.

D.

A. One Patch, 10¾" x 10¾", circa 1890, Pennsylvania, $200.00 – 300.00.

B. Nine Patch Doll Quilt, circa 1915, hand quilted, knife edge finish, good condition, $50.00 – 75.00.

C. One Patch, 13" x 19", circa 1880, made in New England, $100.00 – 200.00.

D. Four Patch, 12½" x 19", circa 1890, the diagonal organization adds interest to this simple design, $100.00 – 200.00.

A. Pieced Star, 16" x 16", circa 1880, New England, $100.00 – 200.00.

B. Evening Star, 10½" x 11", circa 1880, Berks County, Pennsylvania, $100.00 – 200.00.

C. Spools, 10½" x 10½", circa 1900, Pennsylvania, $100.00 – 200.00.

D. Baskets, 13" x 13", circa 1920, machine quilted, excellent condition, front brought around to back edge finish, $50.00 – 75.00.

A.

B.

C.

D.

A.

B.

C.

A. Doll Quilts, 13" x 17",
made for twins in 1915, hand
quilted with an X pattern,
back brought around to front
to finish edges, good condition, $125.00 – 150.00.

B. Circles, 15" x 15", circa
1910, blue and light print
with four red circles, red
binding, plaid back, hand
quilted in triple diagonal
pattern, excellent
condition, $125.00 – 150.00.

C. Wool One Patch,
15" x 22", circa 1865,
Pennsylvania, wool challis
and one cotton double pink
print, $100.00 – 200.00.

A. One Patch and Alternate Crazy Patch, 16½" x 20½", circa 1900, Pennsylvania, excellent condition, $300.00 – 400.00.

B. Preprinted Patchwork from Gilbert and Sullivan Operetta, 15" x 16", circa 1885, New England, within three months of the debut of *The Micado,* this fabric was in print, quiltmaker used it for both sides of this quilt, $100.00 – 200.00.

C. Preprinted Patchwork, 16½" x 20¼", circa 1910, $100.00 – 150.00.

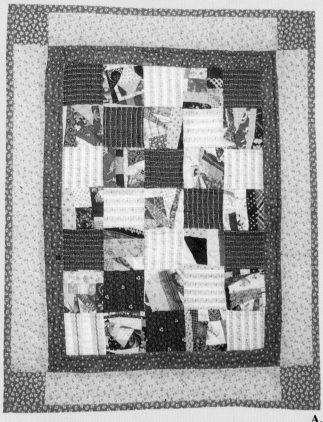

A.

C.

B.

A.

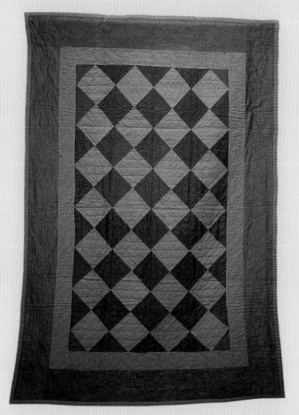

B.

C.

A. Printed Patchwork Crib Quilt, 34" x 45", circa 1910, $275.00.

B. Amish Checkerboard, 38" x 55", circa 1940, Ohio, excellent workmanship, excellent condition, $2,200.00 – 2,400.00.

C. Amish, 10½" x 14", circa 1910, Ohio, Amish doll quilts are rare, $200.00 – 300.00.

A.

A. Amish Brickwork, 15" x 28", circa 1890, Illinois, wool, featherstitching with wool border at one end, $200.00 – 300.00.

B. Log Cabin Courthouse Steps, 17" x 17", circa 1890, many doll quilts are tied, $200.00 – 300.00.

C. Sampler, Tied Comforter, 34" x 44", circa 1900, Paris, Tennessee, embroidered, excellent condition, $1,400.00 – 1,600.00.

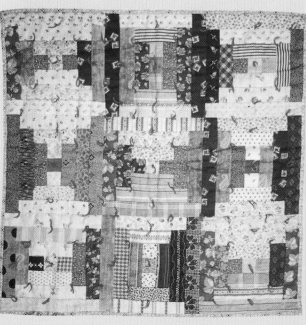

B.

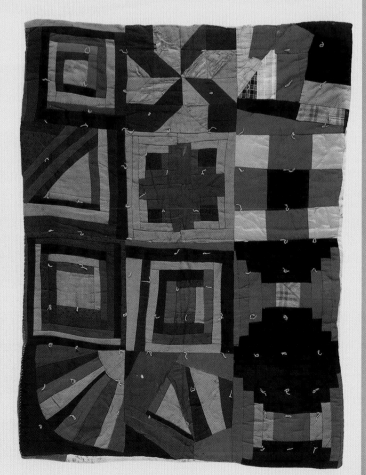

C.

A.

A. Courthouse Steps Tied Comforter, 17" x 17", circa 1890, Pennsylvania, excellent condition, $175.00 – 200.00.

B. Comfort Style Doll Quilt, 23" x 25", 1890, good example of 1890 colors and quilt style, $175.00 – 250.00.

B.

A. Dark and Light,
23" x 26", circa 1880,
Pennsylvania, excellent
condition, $350.00 – 400.00.

B. One Patch Doll Comfort,
9½" x 16", circa 1890, made
with a print of a stork, simple
design was cut to feature the
print, excellent condition,
$275.00 – 325.00.

C. Crazy Tied Comforter,
11½" x 16", circa 1910,
Pennsylvania,
$150.00 – 200.00.

D. Four Patch Doll Quilt
(tied comforter), 11" x 19",
circa 1890, Pennsylvania,
simple patchwork block often
taught to children when
first learning to sew,
$175.00 – 250.00.

E. Silk Crib Quilt,
32½" x 32½", circa 1850,
Maine, wonderful small scale
combination of pieced and
sashed blocks with
Dogtooth border,
$3,000.00 – 4,000.00.

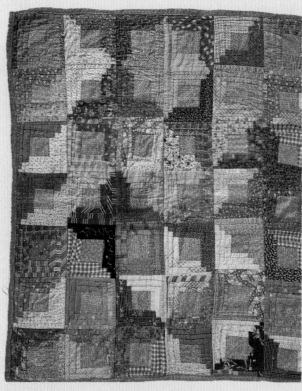

A.

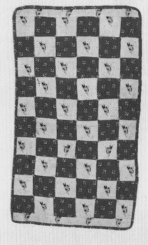

B.

C.

D.

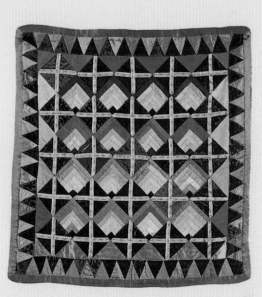

E.

Quilt Tops

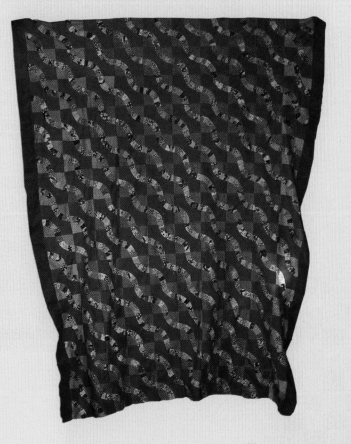

A.

A. Orange Snails Trail,
68" x 84", circa 1940,
Kentucky, poorly
constructed borders,
$50.00 – 75.00.

B. Nine Patch Bars,
74" x 90", circa 1895,
excellent condition, red is
the unifying color that
makes this top attractive,
$150.00 – 175.00.

B.

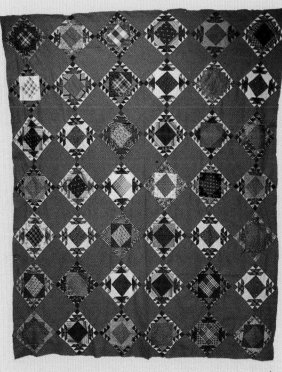

A.

B.

C.

A. Love Entangled,
76" x 86", circa 1890,
excellent condition,
there are 42 pieced blocks,
$375.00 – 425.00.

B. Carpenter's Square,
71" x 72", circa 1890,
Maryland, graphic,
$400.00 – 600.00.

**C. Hexagon Mosaic Friend-
ship,** 74" x 78", circa 1850,
very good condition, a few
stains, signatures are
stamped in each light
hexagon, $350.00 – 450.00.

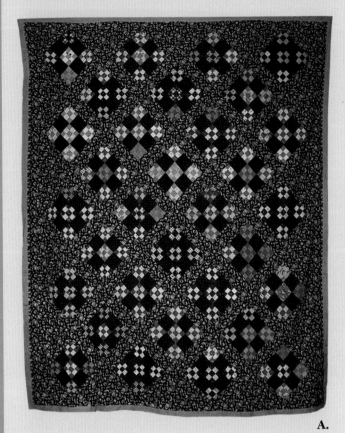

A.

B.

C.

A. Double Nine Patch,
70" x 88", circa 1900, set
on point with print sashing
and border, excellent
condition,
$300.00 – 400.00.

B. Nine Patch, 78" x 86",
circa 1845, excellent
condition, no borders,
$350.00 – 450.00.

C. Arrowhead Puzzle,
72" x 84", circa 1880,
excellent condition,
$200.00 – 250.00.

A.

B.

C.

A. Friendship Star Variation,
68" x 86", circa 1940, excellent
condition, $250.00 – 300.00.

B. Album, 60" x 84", circa
1880, no signatures or dates,
blocks in excellent condition,
however, poor workmanship in
the sashing, $125.00 – 175.00.

C. Mosaic #17, 64" x 91",
circa 1870, good condition,
few stains and soil,
$275.00 – 325.00.

181

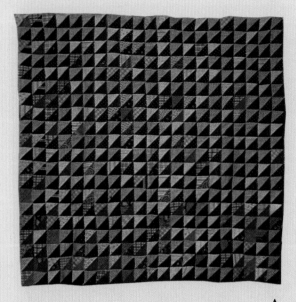

A.

B.

C.

A. Half-square Triangles, 46" x 48", circa 1895, blue crib top, excellent condition, $150.00 – 200.00.

B. Pinwheel Four Patch with Paisley Borders, 60" x 88", circa 1870, excellent condition, $500.00 – 600.00.

C. Nine Patch on Point, 66" x 86", circa 1930, excellent condition, no borders, $225.00 – 300.00.

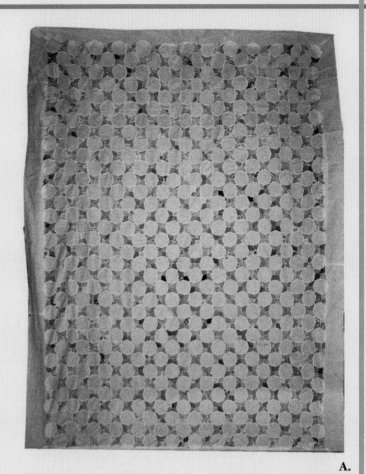

A.

B.

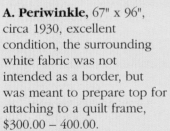

C.

A. Periwinkle, 67" x 96", circa 1930, excellent condition, the surrounding white fabric was not intended as a border, but was meant to prepare top for attaching to a quilt frame, $300.00 – 400.00.

B. Broken Dishes, 70" x 84", circa 1920, excellent condition, $200.00 – 250.00.

C. Double X or Double Pyramid, 78" x 90", circa 1930, small stain, very good condition overall, $300.00 – 350.00.

183

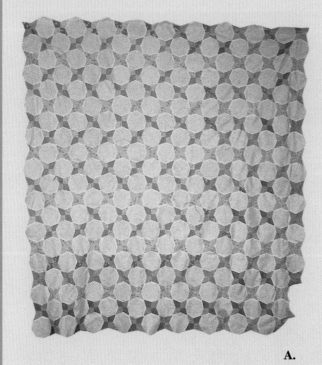

A.

B.

C.

A. Periwinkle or Hummingbird, 59" x 63", circa 1940, excellent condition except two muslin pieces of patchwork missing in one corner, $100.00 – 125.00.

B. Old Maid's Puzzle, 71" x 90", circa 1920, excellent condition, borders, $175.00 – 225.00.

C. Four Patch and Vertical Bars, 81" x 88", circa 1920, excellent condition, no borders, $175.00 – 200.00.

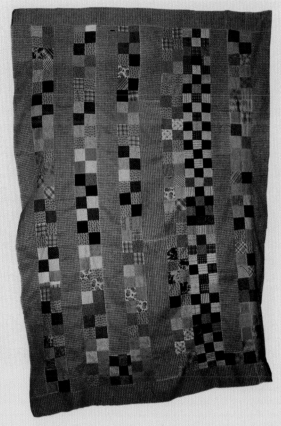

A.

B.

A. Strippy, 60" x 86", circa 1920, excellent condition, poorly constructed, $50.00 – 75.00.

B. Garden Path, 65" x 78", circa 1910, excellent condition, no borders, $200.00 – 250.00.

C. Arrowhead Puzzle, 71" x 73", circa 1910, excellent condition, unusual, $175.00 – 200.00.

C.

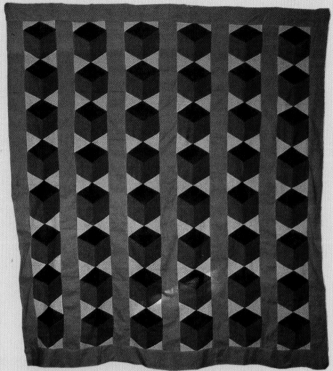

A.

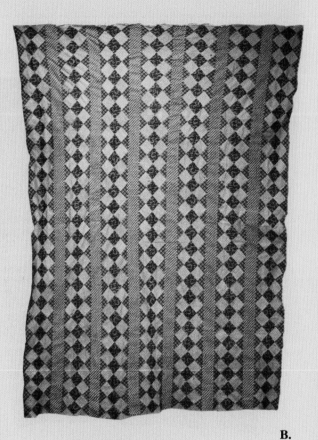

B.

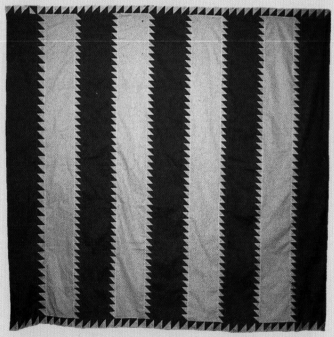

C.

A. Tumbling Blocks,
78" x 84", circa 1900,
excellent condition, very
visual, $300.00 – 375.00.

B. Arrowhead Puzzle,
60" x 88", circa 1880, very
good condition, hangs
poorly and perhaps is a
reflection of the
workmanship,
$75.00 – 100.00.

C. Tree Everlasting,
83" x 76", circa 1920,
excellent condition,
Sawtooth border on top and
bottom, $400.00 – 500.00.

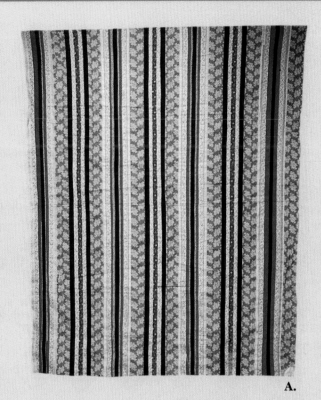

A.

B.

A. Strippy, 69" x 84", circa 1920, excellent condition, made of over 40 strips of fabric sewn together, $125.00 – 150.00.

B. Snowflake, 78" x 82", circa 1890, excellent condition, blue and white is the most popular two-color quilt combination, $550.00 – 700.00.

C. Old Maid's Puzzle, 72" x 93", circa 1890, excellent condition, blocks are placed in a Nine Patch formation alternating with tan blocks, blue and white quilts are becoming harder to find and therefore, the value has risen greatly in recent years, $550.00 – 700.00.

C.

A.

A. Double Hourglass Variation,
70" x 84", circa 1890, excellent
condition, $400.00 – 500.00.

**B. Strippy Construction with
Block Medley,** 47" x 90",
circa 1920, excellent condition,
blocks include Chinese Coins,
Nine Patch, Rail Fence,
$175.00 – 200.00.

B.

A.

B.

A. Jacob's Ladder Scrap,
71" x 82", circa 1950,
excellent condition, no
borders, $150.00 – 175.00.

B. Pattern or Sampler,
59" x 70", circa 1900,
excellent condition, made in
Pennsylvania, very visual,
$450.00 – 550.00.

C. Cactus Basket, 58" x 85",
circa 1875, excellent
condition, borders. "plain"
blocks are black and white
check, $375.00 – 450.00.

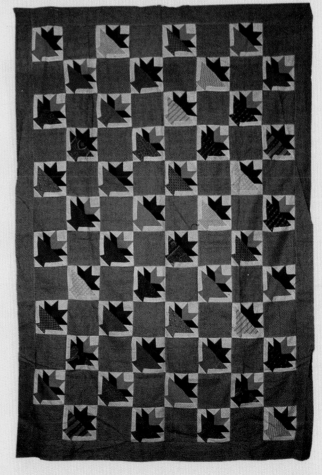

C.

A.

B.

C.

A. Flower Pots, 69" x 78",
circa 1870, poor condition,
nine blocks with a folk art
feel, fugitive green dye,
$100.00 – 125.00.

**B. Trip around the World or
Grandmother's Dream,**
66" x 68", circa 1890,
Pennsylvania, excellent
condition, very graphic,
$250.00 – 350.00.

**C. Red and White
Fundraiser "Wheels,"**
70" x 85", circa 1915,
excellent condition, very
poorly constructed,
$150.00 – 200.00.

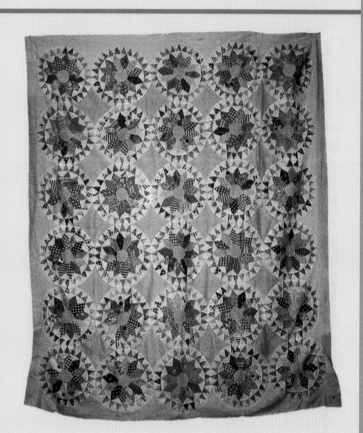

A.

B.

A. The Hex Stars, 64" x 78", circa 1940, excellent condition, borders poorly attached, high degree of difficulty in executing this pattern, $300.00 – 400.00.

B. Star of Bethlehem, 70" x 90", circa 1950, excellent condition, 20 blocks, pattern has a high degree of difficulty, $200.00 – 250.00.

C. Tulips, 78" x 88", circa 1920, Indiana, the appliqué scallop border adds to the beauty of this appliqué top, $200.00 – 300.00.

C.

A.

A. Mosaic #21, 70" x 82", circa 1840, Maryland, ombre print and the brown madder prints give clues to the age of this top, $200.00 – 400.00.

B. Medallion, 58" x 60", circa 1830, Pennsylvania, unusual settings and borders appeal to some collectors, the early prints and colors in this top are of interest, $300.00 – 500.00.

B.

A.

B.

A. Amish Straight Furrow,
96" x 97", circa 1950, Indiana, excellent condition, $150.00 – 250.00.

B. Thousand Pyramids,
74" x 84", circa 1870, pieced by an "old maid" from Maine, good example of the variety of prints available after the Civil War, typical of the charm quilts made during the last quarter of the nineteenth century, $100.00 – 300.00.

A.

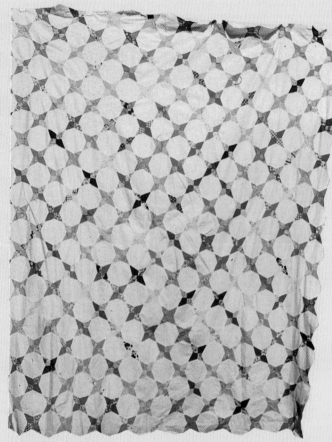

B.

C.

A. Star and Octagon, 72" x 84", circa 1930, Indiana, fabrics used are typical of this time period; however, the pattern is somewhat unusual, $200.00 – 300.00.

B. Periwinkle, 78" x 88", circa 1930, Indiana. This is one of the patterns with many names — Snowball, Pontiac Star, Arkansas Snowflake, and Hummingbird. $200.00 – 300.00.

C. Daffodils, 83" x 92", circa 1920, Texas. The solid colors and floral appliqué patterns of the 1920s are more simple than the ones from a century earlier. $100.00 – 200.00.

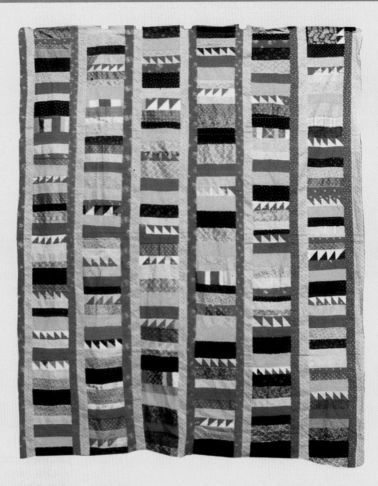

A.

B.

A. Roman Coins Variation,
68" x 80", circa 1890, patchwork strips used in place of
plain strips make this a
variation colors are dramatic
also, $100.00 – 200.00.

B. Grandmother's Dream,
72" x 72", circa 1890,
Pennsylvania, dark color
scheme is very characteristic
of fabric choices by
Pennsylvania quiltmakers,
$250.00 – 350.00.

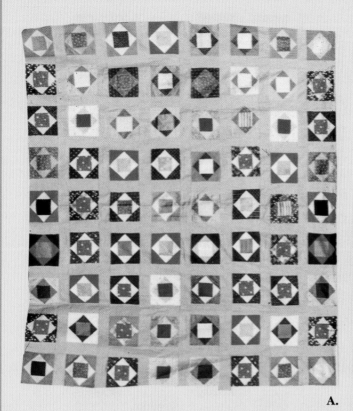

A.

B.

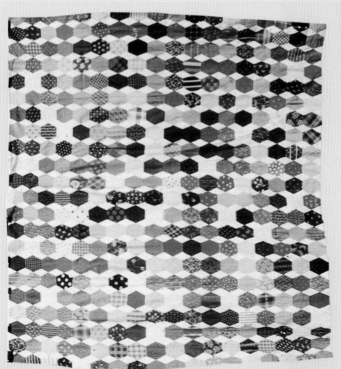

C.

A. Economy Patch,
64" x 70", circa 1890,
Indiana. Many patterns were
used for patchwork quilts
from 1890 on. This is one of
the more popular,
$100.00 – 200.00.

B. Basket Lattice, 67" x 67",
1900 – 1930, Indiana, rare
find, $200.00 – 300.00.

C. Beg and Borrow Charm,
74" x 80", circa 1880,
Massachusetts, contains a
great selection of prints,
checks, and plaids, from the
last quarter of the nineteenth
century, $200.00 – 400.00.

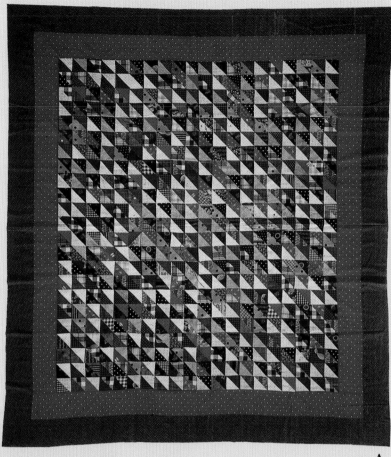

A.

A. Mosaic #17, 85" x 97", 1875 – 1900, Pennsylvania. Scrap quilt tops with good graphics are always in demand. $250.00 – 350.00.

B. Sawtooth Star, 60" x 60", circa 1880, Kentucky, fabrics and setting fabrics used are typical for this decade, $100.00 – 200.00.

B.

A.

A. Currants and Poinsettia,
78" x 82", circa 1885, good graphics, but is damaged due to the harsh mordants used in printing the black dot on the red fabric, $100.00 – 200.00.

B. Six-pointed Stars,
66" x 88", circa 1940, Post, Texas. The use of solids with prints is characteristic of the 1930s and 1940s quilts. $150.00 – 250.00.

B.

A.

B.

A. Wild Goose Chase,
64" x 72", circa 1870,
Massachusetts, by varying
the blocks, the design has
more visible interest,
$100.00 – 300.00.

B. Log Cabin, 68" x 78",
circa 1870, pieced by an "old
maid" from Maine, two tops
from same quiltmaker will
contain many of the same
fabrics, the ones that differ
will define the time period,
$100.00 – 300.00.

199

Quilt Blocks

A. **Appliqué,** 12", New York, 1840, original design, $60.00.

B. **Appliqué and Reverse Appliqué ,** 34", Pennsylvania, 1860, original design, $75.00.

C. **Appliqué and Reverse Appliqué,** 24", 1860, Pennsylvania, original design, $95.00.

D. **Appliqué, Honey Bee Variation,** 15", 1860, Ohio, $50.00.

A.

C.

B.

D.

A.

B.

C.

D.

A. Appliqué Rose of Sharon, 15", 1860, Pennsylvania, $40.00.

B. Appliqué Tulip, 10", 1860, Pennsylvania, $20.00.

C. Appliqué Rose Wreath, 16", 1930, Ohio, ten blocks in set, $30.00 ea.

D. Appliqué Tulip, 20½", 1930, Pennsylvania, $15.00.

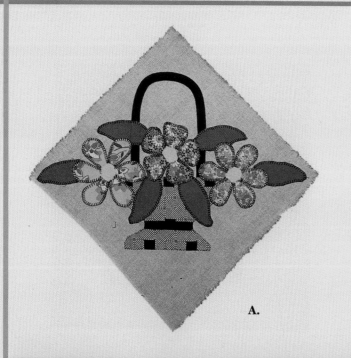

A.

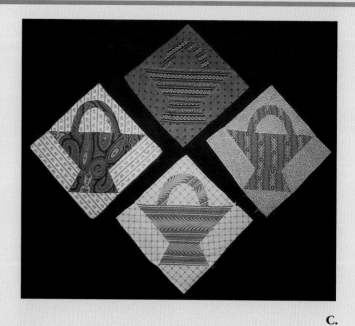

C.

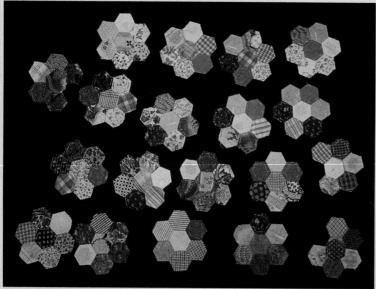

B.

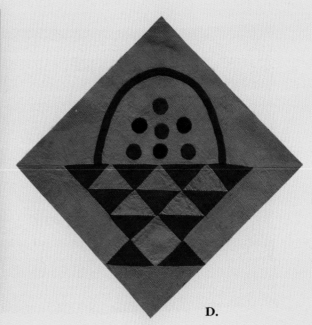

D.

A. Appliqué Basket, 11½",
1940, buttonhole stitch,
Tennessee, 19 in set, $95.00.

B. Hexagon Mosaic Blocks, 4",
1840, New England, English
pieced, chintzes, and early
fabrics, 19 in set, $45.00.

**C. Pieced and Appliqué
Baskets,** 9½", 1870,
Pennsylvania, five in set, $38.00.

**D. Pieced and Appliqué
Basket and Cherries,** 9½",
1860, Ohio, $15.00.

A.

B.

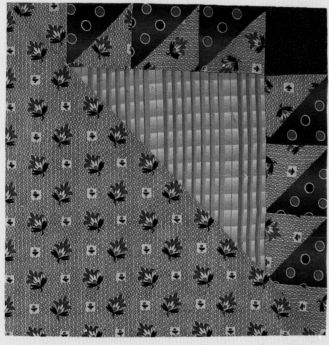

C.

D.

A. Pieced and Appliqué, 9",
1875, Pennsylvania, Tea Leaf,
$18.00.

B. Pieced Basket, 9", 1880,
Pennsylvania, $5.00.

C. Pieced Little Sawtooth,
6", 1850, Massachusetts, 16 in
set, $45.00.

D. Hourglass, 9", 1840, New
England, nine in set, $45.00.

A.

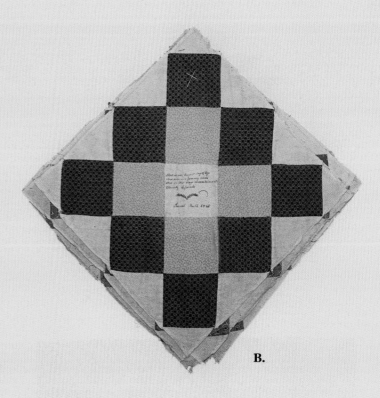

B.

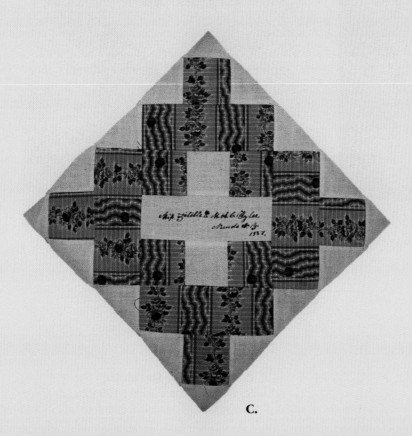

C.

A. Signature Block, 6½",
1840, New England, signed
Austreas J. Miner, $12.00.

B. Album Block, 11", 1845,
Philadelphia, Pennsylvania,
signed Sarah Ruth, 10 in set,
$100.00.

C. Album Block, 9½", signed
1861, New York, 20 in set,
$150.00.

A.

B.

C.

D.

A. Evening Star, 10", 1870,
Pennsylvania, 10 in set, $50.00.

B. Sunflower, 9" diam., 1840,
New England, $25.00.

**C. Album Block Center, Corner
Blocked with Variable Stars,**
23", 1840, Pennsylvania, $100.00.

D. Sawtooth Square Medallion,
22½", 1850, Massachusetts, $75.00.

A.

D.

B.

C.

A. Signature Block Medallion, 17½" x 20½", 1870, Pennsylvania, $75.00.

B. Eight Pointed Star, 9", 1860, Massachusetts, $5.00.

C. Solomon's Temple Variation, 12", 1880, Pennsylvania, block has original template pinned to it, $15.00.

D. Star Variation, 12", 1880, Pennsylvania, 18 in set, $95.00.

A.

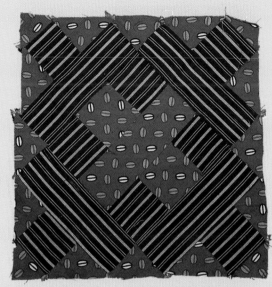

B.

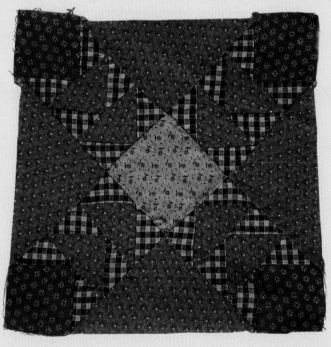

C.

D.

A. Goose in the Pond, 18",
1880, Pennsylvania, $25.00.

B. Signature Block, 10",
1875, Pennsylvania, $7.50.

C. Odd Fellows Block, 8",
1880, Pennsylvania, $10.00.

D. Nine Patch, 9", 1880,
Pennsylvania, $3.00.

A.

B.

C.

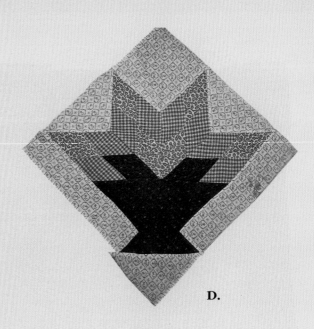

D.

A. Nine Patch, 9", 1890,
Pennsylvania, cheater cloth,
$3.50.

B. Evening Star, 9", 1870,
Pennsylvania, $4.00.

C. Endless Chain, 20½",
1940, Pennsylvania, $20.00.

D. Basket, 14½", 1910, New
England, $15.00.

A.

B.

A. Churn Dash, 10½",1880, Pennsylvania, $4.00.

B. Corn and Beans, 7½", 1880, Pennsylvania, 28 in set, $85.00.

C. House Block, 15", 1880, Pennsylvania, $20.00.

D. House Block, 15" x 17", 1880, Pennsylvania, $25.00.

C.

D.

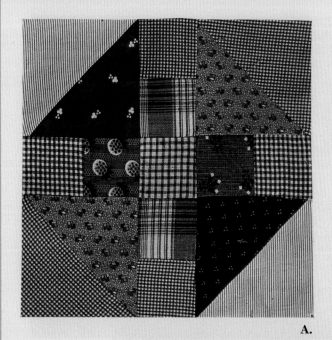

A.

B.

C.

A. Churn Dash, 9", 1890, Pennsylvania, $7.50.

B. Red Work, 8½", 1890, Pennsylvania, embroidered, $3.00 ea.

C. Ocean Waves, 5" x 7", 1890, Pennsylvania, $6.50.

D. Green Work, 9", 1890, Pennsylvania, $3.00.

D.

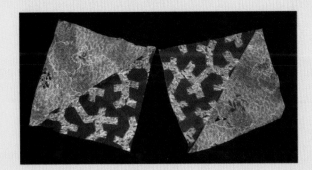

A.

B.

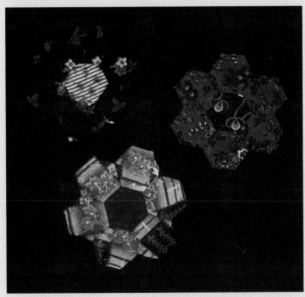

C.

A. Half-square Cotton Triangle Blocks, 5", 63 total, circa 1830, excellent condition, $150.00.

B. Cotton or Chintz Star Blocks, 5½", circa 1835, 35 total, excellent workmanship, excellent condition, rare, $300.00.

C. 5" Hexagon Mosaic Blocks, circa 1845, wool challis, English paper pieced with handwritten letters (including dated material) used as foundations, excellent workmanship, excellent condition, 40 total, $150.00.

D. Cigar Silks, circa 1895, excellent condition, 36 total, $60.00.

D.

A.

B.

C.

D.

A. 7" Antimony Orange and Early Madder Star Blocks, 1860, 65 total, cotton, excellent workmanship, excellent condition, $300.00.

B. 12" Embroidered Redwork Block, dated 1892, cotton, excellent workmanship, excellent condition, only one, $35.00.

C. Turkey Red Embroidered Blocks of Young Girls and Women, circa 1910, cotton, 11" square, 10 total, excellent condition, $35.00.

D. Oak Leaf and Reel, 15" cotton blocks, circa 1830, ink stamped with name and leaves, 12 total, excellent workmanship, excellent condition, rare, $400.00.

A.

B.

C.

A. Roman Cross, 12" block, circa 1870, cotton, madder prints and green with black and yellow print, excellent condition, six total, $15.00 each.

B. Broken Dishes, 8", circa 1860, excellent condition, seven total, $40.00.

C. Bowtie, 7½" block, circa 1890, excellent workmanship, excellent condition, great assortment of period prints, 25 total, $200.00.

A.

A. Jack in the Pulpit, circa 1890, beautiful 1880s and 1890s fabrics, 25 total, excellent workmanship, excellent condition, $300.00.

B. Crazy Patch, 14" block, 1912, probably meant as pillow cover, embroidered Jan. 1912, excellent workmanship, excellent condition, one total, $25.00.

C. Nine Patch, 4" blocks, circa 1900, woven plaids, checks, indigos, and shirtings, excellent workmanship, excellent condition, 43 total, $150.00.

D. Nine Patch, 13" blocks, circa 1900, good workmanship, excellent condition, seven total, $40.00.

B.

D.

C.

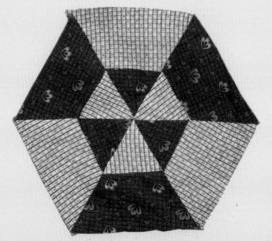

A.

B.

C.

D.

A. Wrench, 5" block, circa 1860, excellent condition, handwoven checks, six total, $45.00.

B. Checkerboard, 14" block, circa 1870, madder prints, excellent workmanship, some dye migration, one total, $20.00.

C. Rosebud, 10½" block, circa 1870, double pink and green, good workmanship, some staining, one total, $10.00.

D. Hexagon, 7½" across, circa 1880, excellent workmanship, excellent condition, 31 total, $125.00.

A.

B.

C.

A. Mourning Prints, Triangle Blocks, 12" on a side, circa 1880, excellent condition, 17 total, $150.00.

B. Mrs. Hoover's Colonial Quilt, circa 1890, "X's" containing 16 patch in intersections and patches on point in legs, squares are 1¼", eight total, $95.00.

C. 4½" Wings in a Whirl blocks set with Nine Patch within print in alternating squares, circa 1890, nine total, $175.00.

D. Appliqué Tulip with Chain Stitching Embroidery on All Edges, 16" , circa 1930, excellent condition, one total, $15.00.

D.

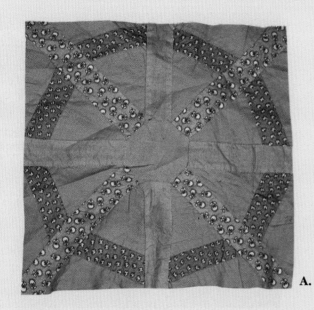

A.

B.

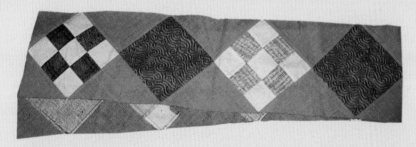

C.

D.

A. Spider with Northern Lights, or Wagon Wheel, or Wheel Friendship Block, 10½", circa 1920, excellent workmanship, excellent condition, eight total, $100.00.

B. 7" x 8" Blocks of Split Nine Patch, circa 1900, good workmanship, excellent condition, 37 total, $180.00.

C. Long Row of Patchwork, 6" x 48", circa 1880, excellent workmanship, excellent condition, $40.00.

D. Sunflower, pieced 14" blocks, circa 1950, beautiful colors, excellent workmanship, good condition, few stains, 42 total, $250.00.

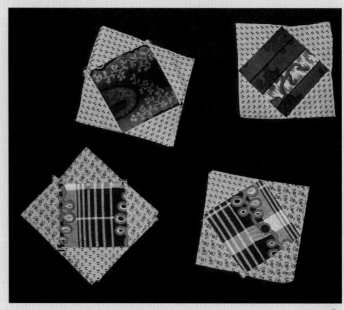

A.

B.

C.

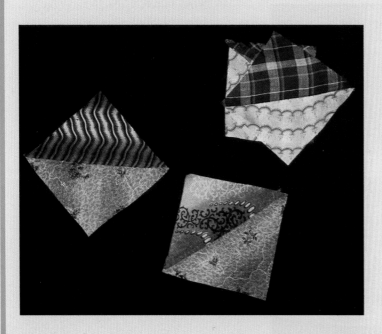

A. Unusual Appliqué Floral Block, 20", circa 1930, excellent workmanship, excellent condition, one only, $20.00.

B. 3" Economy Patch Blocks, various garish yellow print grounds, circa 1835, excellent workmanship, excellent condition, 12 total, $30.00.

C. Half-square Triangle, 4½" blocks, circa 1830, excellent condition, four total, $18.00.

D. Half-square Triangle, 5" blocks, circa 1830, excellent workmanship, excellent condition, 16 total, $80.00.

D.

A.

C.

B.

D.

A. 9" Nine Patch Blocks,
circa 1895, some edge
stitches visible which would
indicate that these probably
were part of a quilt top,
fair/good condition, 31 total,
$100.00.

**B. 8" Nine Patch Blocks in
Early Brown Prints,**
circa 1850, excellent
workmanship, excellent
condition, six total, $35.00.

C. 8" Sixteen Patch Blocks,
circa 1900, fair condition,
eight total, $35.00.

D. 9" Nine Patch Blocks,
circa 1900, excellent "as
new" condition, 24 total,
$100.00.

A.

B.

C.

A. Crosses and Lasses, 8½"
blocks, circa 1920, excellent
workmanship, excellent
condition, nine total, $55.00.

B. Pieced Triangle Units,
circa 1880, 11" on short
sides, good workmanship,
excellent condition, 81 total,
$180.00.

**C. One Half of Eight-point-
ed Star Blocks,** circa 1840,
excellent workmanship,
some staining, seven total,
$35.00.

A.

B.

A. Crazy Patch, 4½" x 5½"
pieced rectangle units, circa
1890, 159 total, $300.00.

**B. 8" Nine Patch with Four
Patch Centers,** circa 1900,
excellent workmanship,
excellent condition,
$8.00 each.

C. Nine Patch Blocks, 7½",
assorted prints, excellent
workmanship and condition,
42 total, $5.00 each.

C.

Sharon Newman is a recognized authority on nineteenth and twentieth century quilt patterns. Her personal quilt collection spans two centuries of quiltmaking. Sharon enjoys making quilts that replicate antique quilts. She is a quilt workshop teacher, lecturer, judge, and appraiser. She may be reached at P.O. Box 94594, Lubbock, Texas, 79493, or by phone or fax at 806-792-1691. E-mail vpsln@ttu.edu.

Bobbie Aug is a collector of antique quilts, as well as art quilts. As a quiltmaker, she enjoys making art quilts as well as those that "touch our roots," meaning traditional quilts. Her quilt show judging and appraising experiences have fine tuned her ability to recognize expert workmanship, technique, and unique qualities she wants represented in her quilt collection. To contact her for class and lecture information: Bobbie A. Aug, P.O. Box 9654, Colorado Springs, CO 80932. Fax: 719-632-9210. E-mail qwlt-pro@uswest.net.

Gerald Roy comes to quiltmaking from a fine art background. After receiving an MFA in painting, he taught art for 10 years in Oakland, CA. Growing up in Massachusetts, he developed a deep love and appreciation for American antiques. Eventually he and his late partner, Paul Pilgrim, opened a gallery on the west coast. Ever since his first serious quilt purchase in 1969, Gerald has been involved in an all-consuming quest to collect the finest examples of quilts that exemplify the unique esthetic nature of the maker. Now, relocated back on the east coast, the quest continues. To contact Gerald about judging, teaching, or lecturing information: P.O. Box 432, Warner, NH 03278.

All three authors are nationally known quilt historians, lecturers, and teachers of workshops about quiltmaking and quilt history. They have been "engaged" in the quilt business for well over 60 cumulative years and have previously sold antique quilts in their own retail stores. Sharon, Bobbie, and Gerald have authored and co-authored more than a dozen books about quiltmaking. In addition to being certified quilt appraisers, they enjoy working as members of the American Quilter's Society Quilt Appraiser Certification Committee, testing and certifying appraisers of quilted textiles. Their love of quilts brought them together.

COLLECTOR BOOKS
Informing Today's Collector

DOLLS, FIGURES & TEDDY BEARS

2079	**Barbie** Doll Fashion, Volume I, Eames	$24.95
3957	**Barbie** Exclusives, Rana	$18.95
6022	The **Barbie** Doll Years, 5th Edition, Olds	$19.95
3810	**Chatty Cathy** Dolls, Lewis	$15.95
4559	Collectible **Action Figures**, 2nd Ed., Manos	$17.95
2211	Collector's Ency. of **Madame Alexander Dolls**, 1965 – 1990, Smith	$24.95
4863	Collector's Encyclopedia of **Vogue Dolls**, Stover/Izen	$29.95
5904	Collector's Guide to **Celebrity Dolls**, Spurgeon	$24.95
1799	**Effanbee Dolls**, Smith	$19.95
5611	**Madame Alexander** Store Exclusives & Limited Editions, Crowsey	$24.95
5689	**Nippon Dolls** & Playthings, Van Patten/Lau	$29.95
5253	Story of **Barbie**, 2nd Ed., Westenhouser	$24.95
1513	**Teddy Bears & Steiff** Animals, Mandel	$9.95
1808	Wonder of **Barbie**, Manos	$9.95
1430	World of **Barbie** Dolls, Manos	$9.95
4880	World of **Raggedy Ann** Collectibles, Avery	$24.95

TOYS & MARBLES

2333	Antique & Collectible **Marbles**, 3rd Ed., Grist	$9.95
2338	Collector's Encyclopedia of **Disneyana**, Longest, Stern	$24.95
5681	Collector's Guide to **Lunchboxes**, White	$19.95
4566	Collector's Guide to **Tootsietoys**, 2nd Ed, Richter	$19.95
5360	**Fisher-Price Toys**, Cassity	$19.95
4945	**G-Men and FBI Toys**, Whitworth	$18.95
5593	Grist's Big Book of **Marbles**, 2nd Ed.	$24.95
3970	Grist's Machine-Made & Contemporary **Marbles**, 2nd Ed.	$9.95
5267	**Matchbox Toys**, 3rd Ed., 1947 to 1998, Johnson	$19.95
5830	**McDonald's** Collectibles, Henriques/DuVall	$24.95
5673	Modern **Candy Containers** & Novelties, Brush/Miller	$19.95
1540	Modern **Toys** 1930–1980, Baker	$19.95
5920	Schroeder's Collectible **Toys**, Antique to Modern Price Guide, 8th Ed	$17.95
5908	**Toy Car** Collector's Guide, Johnson	$19.95

JEWELRY, HATPINS, & PURSES

1748	Antique **Purses**, Revised Second Ed., Holiner	$19.95
4850	Collectible **Costume Jewelry**, Simonds	$24.95
5675	Collectible **Silver Jewelry**, Rezazadeh	$24.95
3722	Collector's Ency. of **Compacts**, Carryalls & Face Powder Boxes, Mueller	$24.95
4940	**Costume Jewelry**, A Practical Handbook & Value Guide, Rezazadeh	$24.95
5812	Fifty Years of Collectible Fashion **Jewelry**, 1925-1975, Baker	$24.95
1424	**Hatpins** & Hatpin Holders, Baker	$9.95
5695	**Ladies' Vintage Accessories**, Bruton	$24.95
1181	100 Years of Collectible **Jewelry**, 1850 – 1950, Baker	$9.95
6039	Signed Beauties of **Costume Jewelry**, Brown	$24.95
4850	Unsigned Beauties of **Costume Jewelry**, Brown	$24.95
5696	Vintage & Vogue Ladies' **Compacts**, 2nd Edition, Gerson	$29.95
5923	**Vintage Jewelry** for Investment & Casual Wear, Edeen	$24.95

FURNITURE

3716	American **Oak** Furniture, Book II, McNerney	$12.95
1118	Antique **Oak** Furniture, Hill	$7.95
2132	Collector's Encyclopedia of **American** Furniture, Vol. I, Swedberg	$24.95
3720	Collector's Encyclopedia of **American** Furniture, Vol. III, Swedberg	$24.95
5359	Early **American** Furniture, Obbard	$12.95
1755	Furniture of the **Depression Era**, Swedberg	$19.95
3906	**Heywood-Wakefield** Modern Furniture, Rouland	$18.95
1885	**Victorian** Furniture, Our American Heritage, McNerney	$9.95
3829	**Victorian** Furniture, Our American Heritage, Book II, McNerney	$9.95

INDIANS, GUNS, KNIVES, TOOLS, PRIMITIVES

1868	Antique **Tools**, Our American Heritage, McNerney	$9.95
1426	**Arrowheads** & Projectile Points, Hothem	$7.95
5616	Big Book of **Pocket Knives**, Stewart	$19.95
2279	**Indian Artifacts** of the Midwest, Hothem	$14.95
5685	**Indian Artifacts** of the Midwest, Book IV, Hothem	$19.95
5826	**Indian Axes** & Related Stone Artifacts, 2nd Edition, Hothem	$19.95
6132	Modern **Guns**, Identification & Values, 14th Ed., Quertermous	$14.95
2164	**Primitives**, Our American Heritage, McNerney	$9.95
1759	**Primitives**, Our American Heritage, Series II, McNerney	$14.95
6031	Standard **Knife** Collector's Guide, 4th Ed., Ritchie & Stewart	$14.95

PAPER COLLECTIBLES & BOOKS

4633	**Big Little Books**, A Collector's Reference & Value Guide, Jacobs	$18.95
5902	**Boys' & Girls' Book** Series, Jones	$19.95
4710	Collector's Guide to **Children's Books**, 1850 to 1950, Jones	$18.95
5596	Collector's Guide to **Children's Books**, 1950 to 1975, Jones	$19.95
1441	Collector's Guide to **Post Cards**, Wood	$9.95
2081	Guide to Collecting **Cookbooks**, Allen	$14.95
2080	Price Guide to **Cookbooks & Recipe Leaflets**, Dickinson	$9.95
3973	**Sheet Music** Reference & Price Guide, 2nd Ed., Pafik & Guiheen	$19.95
4733	**Whitman Juvenile Books**, Brown	$17.95

OTHER COLLECTIBLES

5898	Antique & Contemporary **Advertising Memorabilia**, Summers	$24.95
5814	Antique **Brass & Copper** Collectibles, Gaston	$24.95
1880	Antique **Iron**, McNerney	$9.95
3872	Antique **Tins**, Dodge	$24.95
5607	Antiquing and Collecting on the **Internet**, Parry	$12.95
1128	**Bottle** Pricing Guide, 3rd Ed., Cleveland	$7.95
3718	Collectible **Aluminum**, Grist	$16.95
4560	Collectible **Cats**, An Identification & Value Guide, Book II, Fyke	$19.95
5676	Collectible **Souvenir Spoons**, Book II, Bednersh	$29.95
5666	Collector's Encyclopedia of **Granite Ware**, Book II, Greguire	$29.95
4857	Collector's Guide to **Art Deco**, Gaston	$17.95
5906	Collector's Guide to **Creek Chub Lures** & Collectibles, 2nd Ed., Smith	$29.95
3966	Collector's Guide to **Inkwells**, Identification & Values, Badders	$18.95
3881	Collector's Guide to **Novelty Radios**, Bunis/Breed	$18.95
4652	Collector's Guide to **Transistor Radios**, 2nd Ed., Bunis	$16.95
4864	Collector's Guide to **Wallace Nutting Pictures**, Ivankovich	$18.95
5929	Commercial **Fish Decoys**, Baron	$29.95
1629	**Doorstops**, Identification & Values, Bertoia	$9.95
5683	**Fishing Lure Collectibles**, 2nd Ed., Murphy/Edmisten	$29.95
5911	**Flea Market Trader**, 13th Ed., Huxford	$9.95
5262	**Fountain Pens**, Erano	$24.95
3819	**General Store** Collectibles, Wilson	$24.95
2216	**Kitchen Antiques**, 1790–1940, McNerney	$14.95
5686	**Lighting Fixtures** of the Depression Era, Book I, Thomas	$24.95
4950	The **Lone Ranger**, Collector's Reference & Value Guide, Felbinger	$18.95
5603	19th Century **Fishing Lures**, Carter	$29.95
5835	**Racing Collectibles**	$19.95
2026	**Railroad** Collectibles, 4th Ed., Baker	$14.95
5619	**Roy Rogers and Dale Evans** Toys & Memorabilia, Coyle	$24.95
1632	**Salt & Pepper Shakers**, Guarnaccia	$9.95
5091	**Salt & Pepper Shakers** II, Guarnaccia	$18.95
3443	**Salt & Pepper Shakers** IV, Guarnaccia	$18.95
5007	**Silverplated Flatware**, Revised 4th Edition, Hagan	$18.95
6040	**Star Wars** Super Collector's Wish Book, Carlton	$29.95
3892	**Toy & Miniature Sewing Machines**, Thomas	$18.95
3977	Value Guide to **Gas Station Memorabilia**, Summers	$24.95
4877	Vintage **Bar Ware**, Visakay	$24.95
5925	The Vintage Era of **Golf Club** Collectibles, John	$29.95
4935	The W.F. Cody **Buffalo Bill** Collector's Guide with Values, Wojtowicz	$24.95

GLASSWARE & POTTERY

4929	**American Art Pottery**, 1880 – 1950, Sigafoose	$24.95
5907	Collector's Encyclopedia of **Depression Glass**, 15th Ed., Florence	$19.95
5748	Collector's Encyclopedia of **Fiesta**, 9th Ed., Huxford	$24.95
5609	Collector's Encyclopedia of **Limoges Porcelain**, 3rd Ed., Gaston	$29.95
1358	Collector's Encyclopedia of **McCoy Pottery**, Huxford	$19.95
5677	Collector's Encyclopedia of **Niloak**, 2nd Edition, Gifford	$29.95
5678	Collector's Encyclopedia of **Nippon Porcelain**, 6th Series, Van Patten	$29.95
5618	Collector's Encyclopedia of **Rosemeade Pottery**, Dommel	$24.95
5842	Collector's Encyclopedia of **Roseville Pottery**, Vol. 2, Huxford/Nickel	$24.95
5921	Collector's Encyclopedia of **Stangl Artware**, Lamps, and Birds, Runge	$29.95
5680	Collector's Guide to **Feather Edge Ware**, McAllister	$19.95
2339	Collector's Guide to **Shawnee Pottery**, Vanderbilt	$19.95
1523	Colors in **Cambridge Glass**, National Cambridge Society	$19.95
4714	**Czechoslovakian Glass** and Collectibles, Book II, Barta	$16.95
5528	Early American **Pattern Glass**, Metz	$17.95
5257	**Fenton Art Glass** Patterns, 1939 – 1980, Whitmyer	$29.95
5261	**Fostoria Tableware**, 1924 – 1943, Long/Seate	$24.95
5899	**Glass & Ceramic Baskets**, White	$19.95
5840	**Heisey Glass**, 1896 – 1957, Bredehoft	$24.95
5691	**Post86 Fiesta**, Identification & Value Guide, Racheter	$19.95
6037	**Rookwood Pottery**, Nicholson/Thomas	$24.95
5924	**Zanesville Stoneware** Company, Rans, Ralston & Russell	$24.95

This is only a partial listing of the books on collectibles that are available from Collector Books. All books are well illustrated and contain current values. Most of our books are available from your local bookseller, antique dealer, or public library. If you are unable to locate certain titles in your area, you may order by mail from COLLECTOR BOOKS, P.O. Box 3009, Paducah, KY 42002-3009. Customers with Visa, MasterCard, or Discover may phone in orders from 7:00–5:00 CST, Monday–Friday, Toll Free 1-800-626-5420, or online at www.collectorbooks.com. Add $3.00 for postage for the first book ordered and 50¢ for each additional book. Include item number, title, and price when ordering. Allow 14 to 21 days for delivery.